When Sparrows flew like Eagles

1971 Indo-Pak War of Liberation of Bangladesh

When Sparrows flew like Eagles

1971 Indo-Pak War of Liberation of Bangladesh

(Memoirs of a Signal Officer)

Brigadier MR Narayanan, VSM (Retd)

Corps of Signals

UNITED SERVICE INSTITUTION OF INDIA
NEW DELHI

PENTAGON PRESS LLP

When Sparrows flew like Eagles
1971 Indo-Pak War of Liberation of Bangladesh
Brigadier M.R. Narayanan, VSM (Retd)

First Published in 2020

ISBN 978-81-944659-0-4

Disclaimer: The views and opinions expressed in the book are the individual assertion of the Author in his personal capacity and do not have any offices endorsement. Moreover the Publisher does not take any responsibility for the same in any manner whatsoever. Attributability of the contents lies purely with Author.

Published by
PENTAGON PRESS LLP
206, Peacock Lane, Shahpur Jat
New Delhi-110049
Phones: 011-64706243, 26491568
Telefax: 011-26490600
email: rajan@pentagonpress.in
website: www.pentagonpress.in

Printed at Aegean Offset Printers, Greater Noida, U.P.

ADVANCE REVIEW
"WHEN SPARROWS FLEW LIKE EAGLES"

'When Sparrows flew like Eagles' is unique in many ways. Firstly, this is perhaps the first time anyone has attempted to write about the role of soldier-signallers in the final outcome of a war as they did in IV Corps Operations in 1971 that led to the liberation of Bangladesh. He brings out why signal communication is a force multiplier to win battles and ultimately the War; when timely, how it can avert an unwanted tactical battle and save human lives and war resources. Apart from being a historical narrative, the book has immense value as a military training document. It emphasises human behaviour under stress including psychological dimensions of leadership qualities required at the middle and top management levels during war or warlike situations

The book makes interesting reading, especially for signal officers. The story of the 1971 Bangladesh operations has been written by several officers who took part in them, but this is perhaps the first account by a signal officer. Though the story covers a relatively narrow spectrum of engineering communications at Corps level – operating aspects such as signal centre, exchanges, and ciphers are not covered – it gives an insight into the problems faced by a middle level officer during war and the ingenuity displayed in solving them.

Communications during war have a peculiar characteristic. If things go wrong, they are highlighted by everyone and are often blamed for failures. If things go well, they are rarely mentioned. In the Sino-Indian conflict in 1962, Signals were blamed for debacles at various stages. On the other hand, the Goa operations in 1961 and Bangladesh operations in 1971 were virtually a walk-over for the Indian Army. As a result, communication problems were hardly spoken about. The account written by Brigadier Narayanan dispels this myth. His experiences bring out valuable lessons, which he has highlighted at the end of the book.

Maj Gen V K SINGH
Author of *The History of the Corps of Signals*, Volume II (1939-47)
and Volume III (1947-72)

This is a war story but with a difference.
It is a story by a signal officer bringing out why
Signal Communication is a force multiplier
to win battles and ultimately the war and when timely,
avert an unwanted battle and save human lives.
You will not find nerve-chilling account of infantry
soldiers charging through mine fields against heavy firing;
anecdotes of close quarter battles or beach landings; or
the likes of artillery guns booming, tank or air battles.

CONTENTS

FOREWORD

Lieutenant General SL Mehrotra,
former Signal Officer-in-Chief, Indian Army

Brigadier MR Narayanan approached me recently to write a foreword to his unpublished story *'When Sparrows flew like Eagles'*. It is most creditable that Narayanan who is now past 85 years, decided to publish this book *forty-eight years* after the 1971 War of Liberation of Bangladesh when, he as a signal officer and part of IV Corps Signals, recounts with pride, the contribution made by Signals during this War.

I had known Narayanan intimately from our Army service days. I was the Faculty commander at Military College of Telecommunication Engineering when he did the first post graduate level Telecommunication Engineering Course which he topped with a *'Distinguished'* grade. Immediately after the Course he was posted to IV Corps Signal Regiment and that was when the Bangladesh War 1971 broke out and he was to be 'baptized by fire.'

The IV Corps sector was very large; Sylhet, Badarpur in the North, Chittagong and Cox's Bazar to the South and South East, Mizo Hills to the East. The corps thrust to the West stretched the corps comn to Comilla, Chandpur, and Brahmanbaria and eventually to Dhaka the capital of East Pakistan. From the Corps of Signals point of view, it was a *signal communication* battle that called for leadership, technical competence, innovative approach and anticipation of the moves of formations due to rapid grouping and regrouping in fast fluid battles.

Narayanan who was a major then was in the forefront as engineering company commander where he proved his technical prowess and soldierly qualities in providing infallible signal communications by applying his technical knowledge and expertise to various situations during the War.

'When Sparrows flew like Eagles' is a two layered story; firstly, as *'Reminiscences of a Signal officer'*, the story is unique in as much this is the first time anyone has attempted to write about the role of *soldier-signalers* in the final outcome of a war as they did in IV Corps Operations in 1971 that led to the liberation of Bangladesh. He brings out why signal communication is a force multiplier to win battles and ultimately the War and when timely, how it can even avert an unwanted tactical battle and save human lives and war resources. Secondly, as a military training document, the book emphasises the human behaviour under stress including psychological dimensions of leadership qualities required at the middle and top management levels during war or warlike situations. To emphasise these, Narayanan has narrated several episodes during the initial concentration phase in September 1971 to the outbreak of full-fledged War and the eventual surrender of the Pakistan Eastern Army on 16 December 1971. In one touching episode, he narrates about his few poignant moments with the Pakistani Prisoners of War (POW) after the surrender on 16 December 1971 and how he was able to get the best out of them by treating them with honour and dignity in providing signal communications from Dhaka to Calcutta (HQ Eastern Command) and Delhi (Army HQ) making use of the Pakistan's Eastern Army transmitters and receivers.

Post Bangladesh War 1971, during his Army career, he held various command and staff appointments at the middle management levels. In his last assignment from 1985 to 1988 as a Brigadier, he held the prestigious appointment of Project Director Plan AREN for modernising field force communications. He contributed to successful fielding of AREN during Ex Brasstacks IV in 1987 and was awarded "Vishist Seva Medal-(VSM)." During the last year of his service 1987-88, he worked directly under me when I was the Signal Officer in Chief. He was approved for promotion to Maj General but was superannuated in July 1988 due to age restriction and for want of a vacancy.

I am glad Narayanan has decided to publish his story after more than four decades for posterity. I wish *'When Sparrows flew like Eagles'* all success.

Map of East Pakistan (now Bangladesh)

PREFACE

The events leading to the creation of Bangladesh, beginning with Pakistan Army's crackdown in East Pakistan on 26 March 1971, to the outbreak of full-scale war on 3 Dec 1971 is now a part of history. The campaign was short and swift and lasted about a fortnight, culminating in the surrender of the East Pakistan Eastern Command on 16 Dec 1971

I was then a major posted to IV Corps Signal Regt as Officer Commanding Engineering Company responsible for engineering of the Corps backbone signal communications. I was fortunate to be associated with the operations from the beginning as part of the IV Corps Signals team that included the Corps and the Comn Zone Signal regiments, B Corps Signal Regiment (a newly raised unit in our support), Air Support Signal Unit and the formation signal units under the Corps; all under the dynamic leadership of Brig G S Sidhu, Chief Signal Officer IV Corps.

My motivation for writing this book has been with the following two objectives:

- Firstly, I always felt that IV Corps Signals contribution to the success of the IV Corps operations leading to the liberation of Bangladesh in Dec 71 has not been acknowledged in the Corps of Signals History or any published military or War History books or documents. This is my humble effort towards such recognition.
- Secondly, I am also convinced that we can draw a number of lessons as applicable to our service officers at all levels; perhaps these would be applicable even to the business world in adverse situations.

In the first three Parts, I have attempted to tell my story based on my true experience in those crucial months from Sep through Dec 1971 when the IV Corps Headquarters moved from its permanent location in Tezpur in Assam to Teliamura in the state of Tripura and subsequently moved into East Pakistan- first to Comilla and later to Dhaka the capital; a story that brings out why signal communication is a force multiplier to win battles and ultimately the War and when timely, how it can even avert an unwanted battle and save human lives. I have also narrated a few poignant moments with the Pakistani Prisoners of War (POW) and how we were able to get the best out of them by treating them with honor and dignity.

In the fourth and the last Part under ***'Review, Reflections and Lessons'***, I have acknowledged the role and contribution of other members of the IV Corps Signals Team. I have drawn several lessons that emphasises the human behaviour under stress during war or warlike situations that includes psychological dimensions of leadership qualities desirable at the middle and top management levels.

Since I have ventured to write my memoirs after a lapse of over 37 years, involuntarily, my reflections tend to be philosophical; about the God and human nature; how and why different individuals behave differently in adverse situations; what motivates people to perform beyond their call of duty in war etc.

This being a 'Corps of Signals' story, I have used terms unique to Signal Communications; some of these, I have explained with footnotes or given references to the relevant websites. I have tried to be as authentic as possible, exaggerations if any could be only to sustain the reader interest.

October 2008 **MR Narayanan**
Bangalore

*****

My book "*When Sparrows Flew like Eagles*" has remained unpublished for long years due to reasons beyond my control, mainly due to my deteriorating health with Leukemia (Blood Cancer) which prevented me from actively pursuing with my efforts to publish the book.

In July 2019, I made a resolve to get the same published during my lifetime. I revisited my earlier draft, deleted all operational details retaining only those which are available in the public domain. I have tried to substantially improve the contents and, in particular, make it also a training document to bring out useful lessons on human behaviour under extreme stress and leadership lessons for functional, middle and top management levels during war or warlike situations. For this very reason, I strongly believe that these lessons in leadership would be equally relevant to the corporate world in adverse business environment.

September 2019 **MR Narayanan**

Bangalore

Terms Unique to the Corps of Signals

Sparrow: *refers to a* ***Signal officer***

In the Radiotelephony (RT) procedure followed in the Indian Army, appointment codes are used. e.g. ***Tiger*** *is the code for Commander,* ***Lion*** *for General Staff officer and* ***Sparrow*** *for a Signal officer. These help in concealing the identity of the level of the formation; for instance,* ***Tiger*** *refers to a commander, be he a commander of a Corps, Division or a Brigade. It has become a practice to call a signal officer a* ***Sparrow.***

Signalmanship *is the term simply means sound technical practices to ensure good signal comn viz. Good cable lead-in, terminations and joints, proper earthing, correct radio tuning drills, properly designed aerials, care of the generators and batteries and above all the* ***"will to get through."***

ABBREVIATIONS

Appointments

2IC	Second in Command
CO	Commanding Officer
Corps Cdr	Corps Commander
CSO	Chief Signal Officer
Div Cdr	Divisional Commander
GOC	General Officer Commanding
OC	Officer Commanding
OIC	Officer in Charge
SO	Staff Officer
SO-in-C	Signal Officer in Chief

Army Ranks: Officers

Brig	Brigadier
Capt	Captain
Col	Colonel
JCO	Junior Commissioned Officer
Lt	Lieutenant
Lt Col	Lieutenant Colonel
Lt Gen	Lieutenant General
Maj	Major
Maj Gen	Major General
Nb Sub	Naib Subedar
Offr	Officer
Sub	Subedar
Sub Maj	Subedar Major

Other Ranks (OR)

Hav	Havildar
L Nk	Lance Naik
Nk	Naik

Sigmn	Signalman

Sub Unit, Unit & Formation

Bde	Brigade
Coy	Company
Det	Detachment
Div	Division
Engg Coy	Engineering Company
Fmn	Formation
Mtn Bde	Mountain Brigade
Mtn Div	Mountain Division
Op Coy	Operating Company
Regt	Regiment
Signal Regt	Signal Regiment

Signal Comn Terminology

Comn	Communication
DOT	Department of Telecommunication
DET	Divisional Engineer Telephones
PL	Permanent Line
P&T	Post & Telegraphs (India)
PCO	Public Call Office
PW or POW	Prisoner of War
RR	Radio Relay
RT	Radio Telephony
RTT	Radio Tele Type
RTg	Radio Telegraphy
Radio	Radio
T&T	Telephone &Telegraph (Pakistan)
VFT	Voice Frequency Telegraphy

Miscellaneous

Ops	Operations
Ops Room	Operations Room

Note: Used throughout - **Comn** for Communication; others as required or in full.

Prologue

In July 1956, after completing my Masters in Science (MSc), I joined Military College Dehradun to undergo one year *'Technical Graduates Course.'* On 9 June 1957, I got my commission in the Indian Army, the Corps of Signals. By mid-1966, I had completed about 9 years' service; I was already 32, married with two kids. I had a satisfactory career profile with about 5 years in the field; initial couple of years in *Naga Hills* and later in the *Poonch - Rajauri* sector in J&K. I had adapted well to the Army way of life and looked forward to my future growth.

Like any other officer of my service seniority, I too was preparing for the competitive exam for selection to the *Defence Services Staff College (DSSC)* course; a course not only prestigious but sure-means to get into the *right track* for career growth. Such officers who had qualified on the course suffixed their name with the symbol *'psc'* signifying *'passed staff college.'* Sure enough they were considered experts in all matters relating to military tactics and logistics and what more, they commanded respect. I was determined to get that *'psc'* tag against my name.

Out of the blue, Army HQ Signals Directorate decided that technical graduate officers with MSc qualification like me were really *non-technical* and should attend Signal Officers' Degree Engineering Course or SODE, a 3-year professional course designed for the regular officers from National Defence Academy (NDA) with 4 to 5 years of service in the Corps. I was nominated on the next immediate course commencing in July 1966. I was then serving in 2 Signal Training Centre at Goa. I knew that by close of the 3-year course period, I would have crossed 35 years of age making me ineligible for the DSSC. That would put an end to my ambition of having the 'psc' tag added to my name.

I was thus at the cross roads of my army career," *No longer a technical officer and my aspirations for career growth as a psc officer permanently scuttled."* The Commandant of the Centre at that time (1966) was Col B S Panwar, a gentle and very mature officer and a true leader. When he came to know of my predicament, he gave me a very sound advice,

> *'Develop an attitude to look at every adverse situation as an opportunity and take full advantage.'*

I saw in 'SODE' that opportunity. I was determined to use that platform to enhance and prove my technical competence. My first objective was *to get noticed by my Corps on my technical ability;* later with more experience and with some luck, I would prove that I would be as good as *'psc'* officers in their areas of expertise too.

By July 1966, I found myself at the College of Military Engineering (CME) for part I of the SODE course to re-learn the basic science and engineering subjects. On completion of Part I, we would be moving to *Military College of Telecomn Engineering (MCTE)* at Mhow for Part II to learn specialized telecomn engineering subjects and complex signal equipment. Those three years on the SODE course were the golden period in my Army career because I could relive my *'university days'* without worrying about the travails of day-to-day Army way of life and more so since I had the company of younger course-mates with whom I could savor the typical student life with all their pranks and mischief. With my MSc background, I found the going easy but I still worked extremely hard to ensure that I derived maximum benefit from the course.

From the previous course, at CME, there were a few 'RTUs (Returned to unit) for poor performance. That kept my younger course mates on their toes; quite a few of them used to seek my help in subjects like *Math, Strength of Materials and Electrical Engineering* which caused maximum attrition. This continued even during the second half at Military College of Telecomn Engineering (MCTE), Mhow. By then, I developed a close bondage of camaraderie with every one of them and that continued during the rest of my Army service days. They always addressed me affectionately as *"Naru Sir."*

I topped the Course, with an *Above Average* grade. I was retained at MCTE as an instructor and in that capacity, I earned the respect of my seniors, colleagues and more importantly my student officers. MCTE being our Corps (Signals) alma mater with a large floating population of signal officers on various courses, I began to get known.

Within a year I was nominated on *'Officers' Long Telecommunication' (OLT), a* Post Graduate (Master of Engineering) level course. OLT gave me the opportunity to rub shoulders with a few officers who had already made a mark in the Corps with their technical prowess. Over the next one year, I worked even harder to exceed my SODE performance. Our course terminated in early March 1971. By then, the war clouds had already started to gather. We had to proceed on our postings to our new units immediately. Our course results with the grades had not been finalised when we left. But I knew that I had done well.

I had achieved my first objective, i.e. 'to get known in the Corps for my technical competence.' My next immediate objective was to convince myself and my Corps 'that I am a good soldier capable of applying my technical knowledge to various situations in war.' Bangladesh War 1971 gave me that opportunity. It was early March 1971.

Before commencing with my story, I consider that it would be prudent to firstly give the political compulsions leading to the 1971 Indo-Pak War that resulted in the liberation of Bangladesh. This is covered at Appendix 1: Indo-Pakistan War of 1971. Secondly, appreciate the challenges faced by the Corps of Signals during the 1971 War when we were still in the analog comn era characterised by noisy comn channels and poor quality of service.

Signal Communication Environment during the 1971 War

I strongly urge the readers to move away from the current internet era of digital comn using smart user end devices like PC, laptops, tablets, smart phones and such others for all modes of comn such as voice, data, e mail, image and video transfer. Instead understand the status of signal comn in the late 60s and early 70s.

During the late 60s, signal comn comprised of three modes namely Radio, Line and Signal Dispatch Service (SDS) that were in vogue since the World War (WW) II. The Radio and Line equipment were mostly WW II vintage and bulky, based on valve and discrete components. SDS was based on motor cycle Dispatch Riders (DR) or jeep based live dispatch over short distances and road or rail over long distances. SDS was used essentially for army mail packages and sometimes for 'live message traffic. Digital and data comn had not yet penetrated and tactical satellite comn network was not even thought of.

During the 60s, a new phase of technological metamorphosis was happening when electronics took a quantum jump from valve to transistors and ICs, ASICs LSIs and VLSIs; concurrently there was change from the Analog to Digital Communications. Army Corps of Signals had the foresight to take full advantage of this transformation to conceptualise and introduce Plan AREN (Army Radio Engineered Network) for modernising the field force comn with state of the art, secure and infallible communications. Concurrently, our nominated development and production agencies (DA and PA) initiated the realisation of new range of signal equipment to support the 'Digital Comn' envisaged in AREN. But this was a distant dream that started fructifying only in the late 80s after over 15 years of AREN conceptualisation.

Back to late 60s and early 70s, we were still in the era of analog comn with vintage, heavy WW II equipment. Fortunately, these were being progressively replaced by our own PAs (BEL and ITI) with much lighter and compact transistorised radio and line equipment. Radio Relay (RR) comn was introduced in this period that provided duplex voice comn on Radio and was much sought after in preference to radio com which provided only simplex voice with its (clumsy!) Radio Telephony (RT) procedure of saying 'over' before going to the receive mode. We went to the 1971 war in this environment with a mix of both WW II vintage and improved analog equipment from our own BEL and ITI and thankfully with some RR resources but all signal units were awfully short of these resources.

My story commences in such a Signal Comn environment when we moved for the 1971 War in early Mar 1971.

PART I

1: Move to War Zone: Teliamura (Tripura) 1971

Every signal communication channel has two ends. Never complain about the other end at any time. Instead take responsibility for the other end too.

—IV Corps Signals Mantra

1

War Threat and My Field Posting: March 1971

It was early March 1971. I was a major in the Indian Army undergoing Officers' Long Telecomm (OLT), a post-graduate level course at MCTE,[1] Mhow. The participants, all majors with 10 to 12 years of service included such stalwarts like Yogi Narula the genius, Verma the undisputed wizard of signal equipment and Malay Ghosh an all-round brilliant officer and a dependable colleague who later rose to hold the high office of the Signal Officer in Chief. The competition among us was healthy and close and I managed to remain ahead of them.

It was a Saturday afternoon; I was in the officers' mess sipping a cold beer, a luxury that we always enjoyed after the whole week of grinding. The course was to finish in a fortnight. We were awaiting our postings. For me, it had to be field, after 5 years of peace tenure at MCTE as an instructor and then as a student. I was also due for a regimental *appointment*, a prerequisite criterion for my further promotion to the selection grade of 'Lieutenant Colonel'.

Major Anil Kumar my project teammate rushed in excited, shouting, "Sir, the posting orders are out. You are going to Tezpur to IV Corps Signal Regiment. Maj Ghosh is going to the IV Corps Headquarters (Signals Branch)." Well, that put an end to my anxiety, as the news was as expected. I was also happy that Malay Ghosh was also posted to Tezpur as Staff Officer to Chief Signal Officer (CSO) IV Corps. We had known each other since young officer's (YO) days and over the years had developed a healthy professional association and mutual respect.

Tezpur being a field station, I had to leave behind my wife and two small children in the separated family quarters at Mhow. We were also expecting our third child, due sometimes in early August.

Malay also left behind his wife and two kids; the younger one was just a month old. We both travelled together to Tezpur sometimes in mid-March 1971. IV Corps Signal Regiment looked a good field station posting. The Regiment was well established, the signal comn installations like signal center, exchange, transmitter and receiver stations were well planned and established over a period of time. The unit accommodation was good. The conditions were as good as any peace station. And all said and done, only the absence of families was felt. My Commanding Officer (CO) was Lieutenant Colonel Harkrishan, a smart looking officer with a fetish for physical fitness. Major I C Singal was the other senior major who had been posted recently just before me also for his criteria reports. The impression I got from him and other officers was that Colonel Harkrishan was a hard task master; knew how to extract work from his officers and keep them on their toes.

He liked his key officers to be always around him when he was in the unit; when away, he wanted them present in the unit to "hold the fort" in his absence. In short, he didn't like his officers being away from the unit on leave, temporary duty or otherwise. My first meeting with my CO was in his office and it went thus:

> *"You are coming to a field unit after almost 5 years of peace tenure. Hope you haven't forgotten your soldiering."*
>
> *"Sir, my first posting was in Naga Hills, followed by a full tenure in J&K in Rajauri and Poonch. That was almost 5 years in the field, in my 12 years service".*
>
> *CO: "Hmm, our new CSO[2] is Brigadier Gurdyal Singh Sidhu. Have you ever served under him?"*
>
> *"No Sir."*
>
> *CO: "He is a professional soldier and known to be very strict. He isn't going to be impressed with your academic and theoretical knowledge; so am I. You have to prove on ground what it is to provide reliable comn."*
>
> *"Sir, I will try my best."*
>
> *CO: "Your best may not be good enough."*

Here I am; I have come for my criteria reports. My CO has not given me much hope; my CSO is still an unknown identity; their appraisal reports are to decide my future, whether I move up in the selection grade or suffer the ignominy of a superseded officer. I settled down in my new appointment as *'Officer Commanding Engineering Company'*. I was responsible for the voice and telegraph trunk comn to my formation. After about a week after joining the unit, my CO called me to accompany him to the Corps HQ. I was to be seen by our Corps Commander, Lt Gen Sagat Singh. He had called me essentially to congratulate me personally on seeing my OLT course report indicating "Distinguished" grade.[3]

By mid-May (1971), my CO proceeded on 2 months annual leave, ensuring all his key officers were in the unit to *'hold the fort in his absence!'* My CSO, I was told, was also on annual leave and expected to join duty by early June (1971).

During this period, ever since the Pakistan Army crackdown in end April 1971, a lot was happening inside East Pakistan. There was also a large influx of refugees across the border into India. War with Pakistan had become imminent and was expected to break out by Nov or early Dec. We used to hear a lot about the 'preparations' for the war; but because of very high secrecy, we could hardly get any information on the activities related to our Corps build up.

There was hectic activity in the Corps HQ and lot of moves of officers at all levels to the Tripura State bordering East Pakistan. We, from the Signal Regiment didn't come to know much of the happenings. I was too busy with my regimental routines and hardly had any occasion to meet *Malay Ghosh*. Early June, the CSO rejoined from leave; My CO also rejoined from leave a little later.

Late July, I availed some leave to be with my wife at the time of the arrival of our third child. On 5 August, the baby was born. It was a boy.

I immediately sent a telegram to my CO.

I got a reply on 10 August (1971). The telegram read, *"Congratulations. Rejoin Unit forthwith."* I returned to Tezpur leaving behind my wife with a two-week-old baby and my other two kids, 7 and 5 years in the separated family quarters at Mhow.

During June-July, we were told that the CSO and Malay Ghosh as part of the Corps HQ team had gone from Tezpur to some unspecified location close to Agartala *in Tripura* near the East Pakistan border.

I have given a brief account of the happenings during this period.[4] This account is based on my interactions with Malay Ghosh later after reaching Teliamura in early Sep 1971. This will give an idea of the efforts made at the designated Main Corps HQ location at Teliamura for the build-up of the signal comn, in an underdeveloped area with little or no comn infrastructure.

NOTES

1. MCTE: Military College of Telecomm Engineering- the alma mater of the Corps of Signals situated at Mhow, MP India
2. CSO Corps: Chief Signal Officer of a corps is responsible for all the formation signal communication within the corps sector. The corps signal regiment is a major resource under him to support the corps HQ for voice and telegraph comn including manning the signal center for message traffic and the telephone exchange.
3. The "Distinguished" grade is awarded for outstanding performance on the Course. This gave me the image as a 'technical expert' in all signal comn matters during the War and in my subsequent army career.
4. **Maj M K Ghosh's side of the Story:** In Jun 1971 Maj M K Ghosh SO2 Signals had accompanied the General Officer Commanding (GOC) Corps and the CSO along with a few other senior officers from the Corps HQ to Agartala via Gauhati. They all had travelled in civil dress for secrecy. He was not aware of the purpose of the visit at that time. He along with GSO1 Operations (Ops) Lt Col Mohinder Singh and SO2 Engineers Maj Banerjee, were left at Teliamura, which was a small village in an erstwhile refugee camp vacated because of cholera epidemic. They were to oversee the preparations for locating the Main HQ of the Corps at that location. Malay was specifically assigned the task of liaising with the Post & Telegraphs (P&T) to prepare the groundwork for setting up a comn node at the designated main Corps HQ location prior to the move of Main Corps HQ from Tezpur. As the Signals rep, his job was to ensure before the arrival of the main Corps HQ that the P&T sets up the following important connectivity/facilities;
   - Speech and Teleprinter facilities as per the authorised scales between

Corps and Command HQ, Corps and Army HQ as also Corps and Rear Corps at Tezpur.

- The construction of a VHF Radio Tower at Teliamura for connectivity to Cherapunji and thence to Shillong to enable P&T to provide the requisite circuits as no landline connectivity was possible.
- Extend/improve the speech circuits to Agartala and to Dharmanagar from Teliamura
- Construction of the plinth, ducting, cabling and other works in respect of the proposed 200 Line Exchange and the Signal Centre at Teliamura
- A PL (Permanent Line) route construction, which had started between Teliamura and Amarpur, was to be extended up to Belonia on the E Pak border

During all this time till about July end, he and his colleagues at Teliamura were operating in civil dress and eating at roadside dhabas at Ambasa 14 Km away. The Brigade Signal Company at Agartala had provided him with a Jeep, which allowed him to move about.

2

Move to Teliamura: Sep 1971

In August 1971, IV Corps HQ was ordered to move from Tezpur and concentrate at Teliamura in Tripura situated 45 km from the border with the then East Pakistan (now Bangladesh).

On 28 August 1971, I was leading a convoy of 260 vehicles as part of the Corps HQ move from our present location – Tezpur in Assam to Teliamura. The convoy had jeeps, jongas, 3 Ton and 5 Ton vehicles, ambulances and an assortment of specialist vehicles including some vital comn vehicles. The road journey would take us through the plains of Assam to Gauhati, a climb over Khasi foot hills to Shillong, further steep climbs up to Jowai and thereafter go down the hills to reach the ferry site at Badarpur; ferry crossing over the wild and turbulent *Barak River* a tributary of the Great Bramhaputra. There was no road bridge across the River in those days.

Badarpur to Karimganj was another 100 km where the road grazes the border with East Pakistan; another 100 km to *Dharmanagar* and a further 100 km to our final destination *Teliamura.* The total distance was close to 1200 km and I was to reach Teliamura with a maximum three night stopovers.

Barak River is in northeastern India and eastern Bangladesh, 560 miles (900 km) in length. It rises in the Manipur Hills in northern Manipur state, India, where it is called the Barak, and flows west and then southwest into Mizoram state. There it veers north into Assam state and flows west past the town of Silchar. The river then splits into two branches, the Surma (North) and the Kusiyara (South), which enters

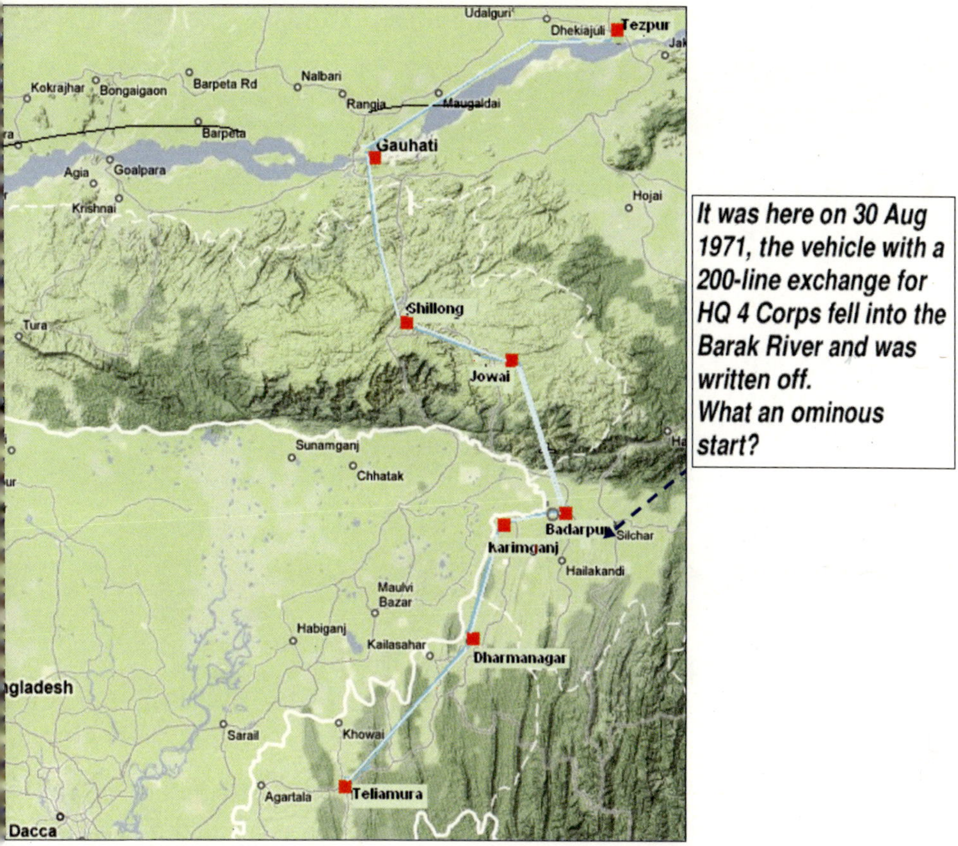

← 150 km → *Courtesy: Google Map*

Bangladesh and turn southwest. The Surma flows past Sylhet in a rich tea-growing valley, while the Kusiyara subdivides into two more branches, both of which rejoin the Surma. At Bhairab Bazar, in east-central Bangladesh, the river enters the Old Brahmaputra and becomes the Meghna River, which flows south past Dhaka and enters the lower Padma River (Ganges [Ganga] River). Many boats can navigate the river as far upstream as Silchar in the rainy season, during the day.

Disaster struck on the second day on our journey from Shillong to Jowai. Our unit mess vehicle went off the road; fell down hill by 50 feet below. The driver and five mess staff were critically injured. I had to arrange their evacuation to the military hospital at Shillong and complete other formalities. That was to be my first battle inoculation. Next day, at the Badarpur ferry, there was this second disaster, a major one; the driver of the vehicle carrying the Corps 200 line exchange while

Barak River and Badarpur Ferry Crossing

Courtesy: Google Map

boarding the ferry, overshot the barrier and fell into the turbulent Barak river. We managed to rescue the driver immediately but the vehicle with the exchange drifted away and sank to the bottom of the river.

Although we managed to retrieve both a little later, the exchange was totally damaged. Damage to a new 200-line exchange for the Corps HQ before the operations was ominous. I wondered, "Why such an ill-omened beginning before the War and why I should get into such a mess?" A deep sense of guilt engulfed me. I started to imagine that every one in the Corps right from the GOC down to the cooks in the langars (soldiers' cookhouse) discussing the mishap and all pointing an accusing finger at me. My morale was low.

"That's the end to my Army career." I thought.

In that gloomy state of mind, as I was drafting a message to my CO about the incident, I felt that I was writing my own *obituary*.

I put behind the day's mishap and looked to the tasks ahead.

It was around 0400 pm 30 August 1971. My morale was low. I heard from behind a familiar and an affectionate voice, *"Naru Sir."* As I turned, I saw *Jimmy Khullar* who was my course mate in Signal Officers Degree Engineering (SODE-18) Course with his characteristic smile below his much-celebrated moustache.

A few words about Jimmy Khullar. I had known Jimmy well for over 3 years during our SODE 18. He was junior to me by over 5 years. He sported a characteristic moustache much similar to that of Field Marshall Sam Manekshaw (and the similarity ends there!). The first half of SODE was at College of Military Engineering (CME) Pune. With my MSc background, I found the going easy. Jimmy and quite a few of my younger colleagues on the course used to seek my help in subjects like Math, Strength of Materials and Electrical Engineering. This continued even during the second half at Military College of Telecommunication Engineering (MCTE) Mhow. They always addressed me respectfully as "Naru Sir" and did so during the rest of my army career.

SODE 18 Course terminated on 29 June 1969. I was posted as instructor at MCTE and Jimmy proceeded to his new unit. Next I met Jimmy was after 3 years, on 30 Aug 1971, at the Badarpur ferry site, on the Barak River, in Assam. (see sketch map). I was then posted to IV Corps Signal Regiment (Regt) and our unit was then moving for the operations (*Bangladesh War 1971).*

Jimmy was then posted to N Communication (Comn) Zone Sig Regt (our sister unit) that had already been deployed in the Sector. The Regiment was responsible to build and maintain hundreds of km of PL in the entire Sector and also take over PL routes owned by the P&T for the Public Call Offices (PCOs). He was camping in that area to oversee the progress on the PL routes. Jimmy just hugged me showing that spontaneous affection. He had come to know of the mishap to the Corps exchange vehicle and could read my mind. He took out a mug, poured large rum from his hip flask and said, "Naru Sir, Have this. You'll feel better."

As I was sipping the rum with him, I felt better; we spent the next 30 minutes or so recalling our SODE days. As he was parting, he smiled and said,

"Naru Sir, this is just the beginning. We will very soon be fighting a War. We have to face many such adverse situations and challenges in the next few months. Very soon this incident will be forgotten. Just don't worry. Keep doing your job and God will be with you."

I am now 74 years (2008) and as I recall those words after over 37 years, I realise that Jimmy the soldier, for those few moments on that evening of 30 Aug 1971, had become my Guru and taught me the essence of "Karma Yoga" of Bhagwad Gita. Indeed, that helped me to re-discover the 'soldier' in me before the operations. I never looked back thereafter.

During the day, I had noticed a tent on the other side of the ferry site across the river with an elevated rod aerial (*Ground Plane Antenna)* next to the tent.

"That has to be a police wireless detachment", I thought. My comn instincts made me visit this detachment. It was around 0400 pm. The radio net was alive and busy; one of the outstations was particularly loud and clear. The police operator said, "Sir that is the Aijal Detachment in Mizoram. It is 120 km line of sight distance from here; since it is at a height, we always have excellent comn both by day and night."

We had lost almost half a day at the Badarpur ferry. I had to make up for the lost time. It was late in the evening. We would need at least 6 to 8 hours to cover the 160-odd km to our next halt Dharmanagar. We would be passing through Karimganj, close to the border.

It was evening 6 pm. The sun had already set and it was dark. The sky was clear and I was desperate. I didn't expect mishaps chasing me but that said I knew we had to move forward; after all we were going for a War and be prepared for even worse. I decided to march the convoy. I ordered full headlights on. I didn't want another accident.

I wondered, "What worse can happen? Face an ambush or enemy shelling from across the border; suffer a few casualties? Let me face these as a true soldier."

It was a plain countryside. A huge convoy of 250 vehicles, stretched over a distance of 10 to 15 km on that night with full headlights on, must have been an awesome sight, particularly for those across the border. Fortunately, there were no further mishaps that night or on the next day. Looking back, I now realise, how dim-witted I was for taking that decision, risking the lives of my men and vital war resources particularly in that Badarpur- Karimganj stretch where the road converges towards the border with East Pakistan. After late night halt at Dharmanagar, we moved early in the morning and reached our destination Teliamura by evening 0500 pm.

Teliamura is a small town in the underdeveloped state of Tripura, around 45 km from the border. Except for the national highway leading to the state capital Agartala right on the border, there were hardly any metal roads. The incessant monsoon rains in the last three months had left the mud roads and tracks with slush and full of potholes. The countryside was rich and covered with tender bamboo growth with a few areas cleared for rice cultivation. I was told that the days were extremely hot and humid. In the evening when I reached, the weather was nice and pleasant I found my way to my unit HQ and in a few moments, I was in front of my CO. It was 31 Aug 1971 and the time was 5.30 pm.

3

Operational Responsibilities of IV Corps and Signals' Tasks

It was 5.30 pm 31 Aug 1971. I was at my Regt HQ at Teliamura in front of my CO in his office tent.

I could see the tension and anger on his face; what followed in the next 10 minutes was *totally one-sided verbal boxing,* I was ducking all the time. I got left, right and center. At the end there was this knock out punch from my CO: "Naru- you have failed as a convoy commander; you have failed us by losing the corps exchange. I shall have no more regard for you."

"That would make a befitting *epitaph* for a soldier who failed." I thought.

I walked out crest fallen, all my past achievements reduced to a rubble and my future surely looking bleak. I felt depressed. I felt that the whole world was up against me.

Even in that depressed state of mind, I did feel sorry for my CO; After all he also must have faced similar wrath from the CSO and the senior Corps staff for loss of the Corps Exchange.

The next day morning around 9:00 am, I was summoned by my CO to accompany him to meet the CSO. At the CSO's office, my CO first went in. I was anxious and extremely nervous as I waited outside. Every minute that passed added to my tension. There was a "buzz". I was asked to come in. I entered. There he was, Brigadier Gurdyal Singh

Sidhu, the person about whom I had heard a lot and now face to face for the first time. He asked me to be seated. (1).

Brig Sidhu was immaculately dressed, looked dignified and smart. He commanded respect with his charismatic personality.

"So, you have lost the corps exchange"? with a stern growl.

I was silent. I tried to control my tears. He ignored that.

"The Signal Officer in Chief (SO-in-C) spoke to me last night. He has promised to send a new 200-line exchange. In addition, he is sending some *carrier and Voice Frequency Telegraphy (VFT) equipment* of the P&T type (2) Can you handle all these?"

Operational Sector IV Corps

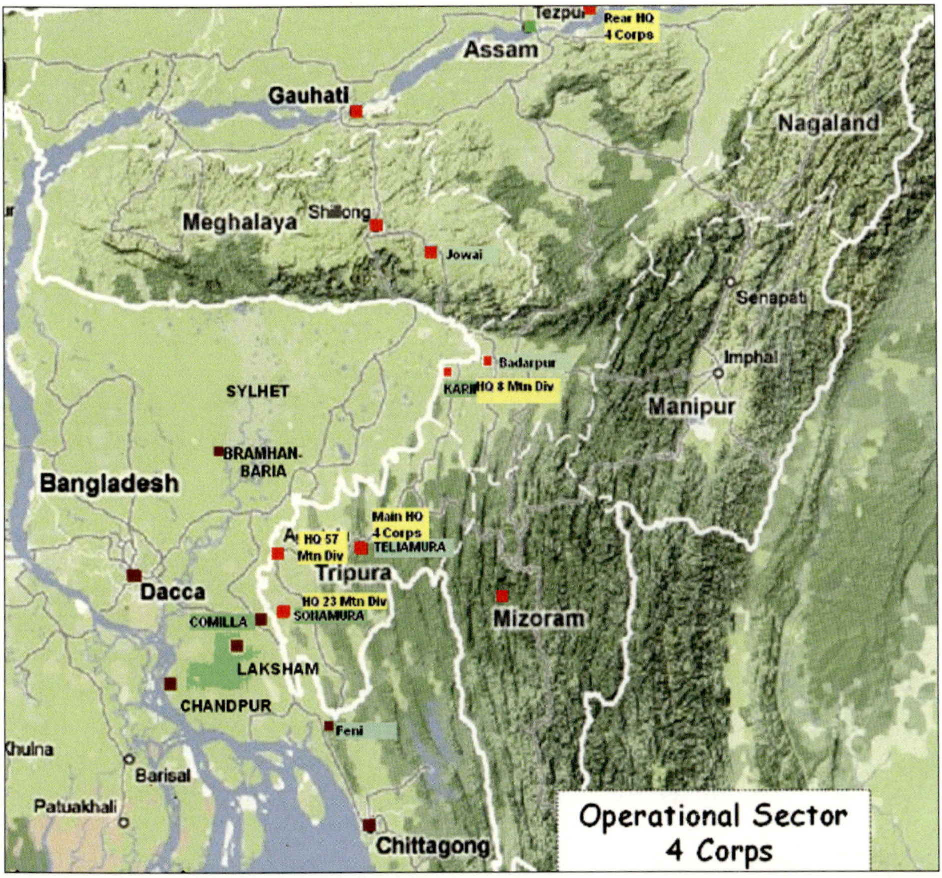

← 150 km → *Courtesy: Google Map*

I kept quiet. He continued, "I want all the comn to be stabilised in the next seven days. I want you to follow the below guidelines:

- First, remember that every comn channel has two ends. I don't want to hear you complaining about the other end at any time. Instead, you shall be responsible for the formation end also.
- Second, if a formation is out of comn for more than 24 hrs, I want you at the other end."

I kept quiet. He said, "You may go. Do meet the SO2 Signals (Malay Ghosh) before you leave." I turned to look at my CO. He was looking the other way. I met Malay Ghosh in his office. It was around 10.00 in the morning (1 Sep). He appeared calm but I could sense that he too was stressed out. Our meeting was more business like. There were none of the usual pleasantries nor was I in a mood to cherish. We spent the next hour or so for me to get an idea of the extent of the operational sector and responsibilities of the Corps, our immediate signals tasks and my Regt's priorities. I have summarised these in ***Note (1).***

As I was taking leave of him, Malay said, "Naru, the new location of the Corps HQ is about 10 km away towards the East. We expect the place to be ready in the next fortnight. There is a lot of preparatory work for us, Signals. Do remember that when the move takes place, we have to ensure that the change-over is smooth with minimal disruption to the comn."

NOTE 1

1 ***IV Corps Operational Responsibilities and Signals' Tasks***

Operational Responsibilities

Besides the defensive task of protecting the Indian Territory from Badarpur in Assam in the north to the borders of Tripura and Mizoram in the south opposition Chittagong Hill Tracts. IV Corps was to destroy Pak forces east of the Meghna and occupy Comilla, Chandpur, Feni and Chittagong (6).

IV Corps sector thus was very large: Meghna River line to the West, Mizo Hills to the East, Sylhet - Badarpur to the North, Feni, Chittagong and Cox's Bazar to the South and South East.

Signal Comn Planning and Challenges

Corps signal plan during the preparatory phase had to cater to its formations in their respective concentration areas. Besides, based on the op tasks given to the Corps, the signal plan had to foresee the likely moves of the formation HQ and build up the signal resources accordingly.

From my unit's (IV Corps Signals Regiment) point of view, we had to plan the signal comn to Main HQ IV Corps and HQ of its three formations viz. 8,23 and 57 Mountain Divisions at their initial concentration locations in Tripura State viz.:

- Main HQ IV Corps — Teliamura
- HQ 8 Mountain Division — Masimpur/Patherkandi
- HQ 57 Mountain Division — Jerania
- HQ 23 Mountain Division — Kakraban

Signals Immediate Tasks

We had to provide speech and telegraph circuits as per scale to Rear Corps HQ at Tezpur, Comn Zone at Shillong, HQ Eastern Comd at Calcutta and Army HQ at Delhi. For this, P&T had just established a microwave link from Teliamura to Shillong with a repeater at Cherapunji since landline comn was not feasible. This vital link was still under observation and not yet handed over. New PL routes were under various stages of construction by our Comn Zone Signal Regt. The comn to HQ 23 Mountain Division (Mtn Div) was also poor since the PL provided by the P&T was substandard and circuitous. The Radio Relay (RR) link due to reasons unknown at that time was marginal. Connectivity to HQ 57 Mtn Div at Jerania, which was close to us, did not however pose any comn related problem.

Note (1.1) 4 Corps Operational Tasks

Besides the defensive task of protecting the Indian Territory from Badarpur in Assam in the north to the borders of Tripura and Mizoram in the south opposite Chittagong Hill Tracts, 4 Corps was to destroy Pak forces east of the Meghna and occupy Comilla, Chandpur, Feni and Chittagong.

—Extract from Official "*War History 1971*", MoD Govt of India, Ch 13: March to Dhaka, p. 552

4

Signal Comn Challenges at Teliamura: Sep 1971

Success is failure turned inside out, the silver tint of the clouds of doubt,
And you never can tell how close you are; it may be near when it seems so far,
So, stick to the fight when you are hardest hit, it's when things seem worse,
That you must not quit.

—Author Unknown

I headed straight to the location of ad-hoc Comn Centre set up by the advance party of my Regt who had reached just a few days earlier. There was a group of bamboo *bashas* (thatched longish huts) occupied by our advance party personnel. I was told that these were part of a *'Refugee Camp'* evacuated much earlier due to *Cholera epidemic*. The Comn Centre was housed in one of the bashas with a center partition. In one half was housed the makeshift Signal Centre. There was a vintage magneto exchange in one corner with a maze of field cables; the noise of the operators responding to the subscribers was unbearable. The Young Officer (I forget his name) on duty was looking helpless. There were piles of messages that had accumulated, all waiting for 'live dispatch' (sending the mail through rail, vehicle and motorcycle dispatch riders) in absence of any meaningful telegraph circuits. Overall it was a pathetic sight.

In the other half of the same basha was the ad-hoc Carrier Station. What I saw here was even more pathetic and things couldn't have been worse. Sub Maj Kalidas, Foreman of Signals who was my Officer Commanding (OC) Line Carrier Part was looking grim and the men, all mechanics most harassed. Every thing inside the room was wrong; no way could we engineer the Corps Comn circuits from here.

I now tried to view the whole situation positively, "I have full 7 days that too in an environment of an impending War, I said to myself, "Why not face the situation boldly and take control? From here things can only get better."

These thoughts brought an eerie calm in me. I decided to take full advantage of the order of my CSO, use the resources of the unit and what I could legitimately demand from the Corps boldly for providing timely and reliable comn. Although I had full confidence in what I could do, but I was apprehensive that my CO may not support me. I decided to act and not wait for any formal or informal approvals that could delay my actions; thus, my loyalty was at conflict but I rationalised with the thought that the corps comn was more important. I needed someone with whom I could share my concerns. Fortunately, Malay Ghosh, my dependable colleague, was there to give me the emotional support if and when I needed. I also knew that I could always reach any constructive comn ideas to the CSO through him.

My first priority was to completely overhaul the ad-hoc Carrier Station. Due to poor *Signalmanship*[1] even a few circuits that were functioning (or non-functioning?) were of poor commercial quality. I decided to dismantle and re-install all the equipment systems.

I called Sub Maj Kalidas, "Sahib, I know you and your boys have been under great pressure in the last 3 days; but these hastily installed systems will not give us any stable comn. I want these to be dismantled immediately and re-installed with proper layout, cable lead-in, terminations and other sound installation practices. We have good mechanics who are competent and well trained and they all understand 'What is Signalmanship.' (1) We will start the dismantling at 1:00 pm. And try and re-install by noon tomorrow. That will give us clear 24 hrs. I will be here with you all for any assistance."

It was noon by then. I asked Sub Maj Kalidas to get all the mechanics and the linemen directly associated to assemble before 1:00 pm after lunch. I rang up Malay Ghosh and told him about my immediate plan, convinced him that a few trunk speeches that are commercial will be directly terminated on the Exchange and there would be no disruption to these channels. I also requested him to contact Lt Col B K Bandari, OC N Comn Z Signal Regt and have someone responsible from the Regt for discussions with me so that we could find some means of improving the noisy PL routes jointly to avoid blaming each other.

I drove down to the P&T Microwave station that was nearby to get an idea on the rear microwave link to *Shillong* through *Cherapunji.* Fortunately, I met one *Mr. Devades*, DET (Divisional Engineer Telegraph) on deputation from the P&T to our Corps Sector. I requested him to accompany me to our Army Carrier Station. When I returned, I was in for a surprise. Lt Col B K Bandari the OC himself had come to interact with me. We had mature discussions.

Mr. Devadas gave a few guidelines for improving the PL trunk routes and also made available his (P&T) linemen to work with the line parties of N Comn Z Sig Regt. He looked at the few P&T type Carrier and VFT equipment that we were trying to install, had them sent to the P&T Microwave station for a quick check up and maintenance. In the next 24 hours, the Carrier Station gave a healthy look with semblance of order restored and the men looking more confident and efficient. What more, the mechanics were focused on their job improving the terminations and labelling them as per accepted technical practice.

Not that speech quality was any better, but we knew that as the PL trunk routes were getting attended to by the P&T and Comn Z line parties, these would progressively improve and we could derive the telegraph circuits too.

The purposeful work started at the Carrier Station was infectious; in the adjoining Signal Centre, the Junior Commissioned Officer (JCO) in charge local lines was smart enough to get his linemen working on the maze of cable wires around the exchange ensuring neat *lead-ins* and sound terminations.

Thus, with a renewed confidence, we had made a positive start towards stabilisation of the comn and improve the ad-hoc comn center; after all we had to function from here for the next fortnight or so.

I spent the next five days with my task teams in the makeshift carrier center.

My CSO's mantra, *"Take responsibility for the other end"* was constantly echoing through my mind; I positioned my best technical persons at the formation ends and also visited the formations. During such visits, I organised training sessions for signals operators and mechanics on the radio, line and RR equipment with emphasis on *'Signalmanship.'* No wonder, the comns started showing signs of improvement.

In these few days, I became aware of that 'indomitable spirit and commitment' in the human beings that motivate them to work, contribute and excel in the face of adversity. I had, now, a renewed confidence that with a committed work force 'the 7 days' time, my CSO's deadline to stabilise the comn was not only possible but we could exceed the expectations, if only such motivation can be sustained by right leadership and professional competence.

During this period, the memory of the exchange vehicle falling into the turbulent Barak River and drifting downstream continued to haunt me constantly leaving me with a feeling of guilt and rejection. I avoided my CO and senior colleagues in the Regt during these 6 days; and surprisingly no one seemed to have missed me either. Perhaps my Commanding Officer (CO), Second in Command (2IC) and Officer Commanding (OC) Operating Company (Maj IC Singal) were too busy with hectic activities that were in progress at the projected Corps HQ location 10 km away in the midst of a bamboo jungle.

My main concern was about the Corps Carrier Station; appropriate location for its security, ease of access and safety from enemy bombing and shelling. We had to cater for a contingency plan to have all vital and important circuits duplicated in an alternate Carrier Station preferably on wheels, secured with full overhead protection (OHP) against possible enemy bombing or shelling. We also had to locate the radio and RR complexes for good comn and easy integration. I wasn't sure if my CO was getting the right technical advice to meet these requirements.

It was on the sixth day (6 Sep 71), I chanced to meet my CO during lunch, I broke my silence to express my concerns about the location of the comn center complexes and their safety. My CO curtly replied, "You better concentrate in stabilising the existing comn. I will ask for your advice if and when needed."

I felt hurt but kept silent.

Fortunately, I didn't have to wait for too long.

The same day evening I was in the carrier center. It was already getting dark. One of my junior commissioned officer (JCO), Nb Sub Dinkar Natu, a diminutive and intelligent JCO rushed in. "Sir, CSO Sahib is outside, he wants you."

Brigadier Gurdyal Singh Sidhu was standing there. I could see even in that dim light, the anxiety writ large on his face. The CSO asked "Naru, any news on the new exchange and the other equipment that the SO-in-C had promised us."

"Yes Sir, we received 12 crates yesterday night. The crates housing the exchange have been sent to the new corps HQ exchange location. We have opened the other crates containing the carrier and VFT equipment, tested them last night itself. They are fine; we are now in the process of installing these in the "Systems Vehicle".

The CSO gave a surprised look. He asked, "Why in the Systems Vehicle." I became nervous; I wasn't sure if I had acted in haste.

"Sir that will give us flexibility – to augment the existing carrier set up or establish an alternate carrier center. We can move it at very short notice when the Corps HQ moves forward or in any other contingency."

He thought for a while. Maybe he found my answer logical. He asked, "When can I see this vehicle with the installed equipment?"

"Any time tomorrow, Sir", I hesitated," But I have to show to my CO first? I haven't informed him as yet."

He came inside and saw for himself a well laid out Carrier Station with mechanics working with zeal. He said nothing but I could see a trace of glow in his eyes.

"Naru, have you seen the new location of the Corps HQ."

I responded hesitantly, "No Sir, in fact I am deeply concerned about the location of the Corps comn complexes i.e. Carrier, RR and the Radio. I am sure these are being taken care of."

He didn't say anything. As he was leaving, he said, "Be ready at 0700 hrs tomorrow morning. I will pick you up from here."

NOTE

1 ***Signalmanship*** is the term that we had learnt during our YO's training. The term simply means sound technical practices to ensure good signal comn viz. Good cable lead-in, terminations & joints, proper earthing, correct radio tuning drills, properly designed aerials, care of the generators and batteries and above all the *"will to get through."*

5

Establishment of Radio Relay Node at Aijal: Sep 1971

"Commanders and the staff are shy to talk on the net radio. They want to make normal duplex telephone conversation. So, we have to plan our Radio Relay (RR) comn well."

—CSO IV Corps, September 1971

The CSO came sharp at 0700 hrs next morning (7 Sep 1971). He made me sit behind the wheels in his jeep and he occupied the co-driver seat. As we were heading towards the new Corps HQ location, he started talking,

"I know you had a rough deal from your CO. For this I am to blame. I lost my temper when I heard about the mishap to the exchange vehicle. This he must have duly passed on to you".

I kept silent and concentrated on my driving over the hilly winding mud road, wet with the overnight rains. The CSO said, "The impending operations are expected to be short and swift. Our success will depend on our ability to provide infallible comn. We have to cover a very large corps sector-Sylhet, Badarpur in the North, Feni, Chittagong in the South, Mizo Hills in the East; towards the West, our thrust could take us to Meghna River line roughly 150 Km from our present location. Corps HQ to the formation HQ distances could stretch to as high as 150- 200 km as the operations progress. The Corps commander is deeply concerned about the comn. We have to deliver."

He was friendly, trying to share his concern with me over the difficult tasks ahead.

"Naru, the problem is that the commanders and the staff are shy to talk on the net radio. They want to make normal duplex telephone conversation. So, we have to plan our Radio Relay (RR) comn well."

He paused and waited for my response. I continued to remain silent. Then the CSO made a statement most unexpected by me.

"We have been trained in the Army all along for the role we are to play in war. We are here now to fight a war. We have to provide reliable signal comn for the success of the Corps operations; we need to find innovative solutions; forget whatever had happened in the past few days and get on with the job. We need technically competent officers like you."

'I couldn't believe what I heard. For the first time in the last so many days, I felt "wanted". I could feel a new enthusiasm surging in me. I felt my confidence returning. I looked at Brigadier Gurdyal Singh Sidhu. I wondered:

> *"How is it that a crisis situation invokes the God from within only a few? While in most, it makes them mere mortals pleading for His mercy."*

I drove silently all the time thinking, "How am I going to live up to the expectations of my CSO? How are we to provide duplex telephone comn to the formations spread over 200 km?"

As we drove further, the road gradient was getting steeper. For the next 3 km or so I was driving in the low gears through the slush and the potholes on the muddy road. Suddenly, the gradient ended and I could see an awesome countryside lit up by the morning Sun; it was carpeted green with tender bamboo growth over a vast stretch of undulating land. Perhaps,Steven Spielberg could have chosen this site for the scene showing the breath-taking countryside of the dinosaurs in his famous movie 'The Jurassic Park.' It was here our new Corps HQ was being located and so was my Regiment. In the next three months, we were to function from here.

For a moment my thoughts drifted down my memory lane to an incident when I was a young officer (Lt) with just 3 years' service.

It was sometimes during the summer of 1961. I was posted as 2 IC of a Brigade Signal Company at Poonch in the J&K. My OC was on leave and I was officiating as the Brigade Sparrow.[1]

On one occasion, in the morning, I was with the BM (Brigade Major); the Brigade Comdr was proceeding to the Divisional HQ at Rajauri. He was on the move; there was a call on D1, the Comd Radio net. The radio link was very noisy. It was the Brigade Comdr from his rover set, "Tiger here. Fetch Sparrow. Over." He was obviously most irritated with the noisy radio link.

BM, "Lion here. Yes, Sparrow here with me." He winked at me and handed over the handset, "Face the music."

I meekly answered, "Sparrow here. Over."

I heard the yell of the TIGER, "What the hell is happening to the comn? Whoever called you 'Sparrow'? Better learn to fly like an EAGLE if you wish to survive in this sector."

Recalling the incident after so many years, I could now appreciate the significance of those spontaneous remarks of the Brigade Comdr.

"May be he was right," I said to myself, ***"I wish we (sparrows) could fly like eagles."***

My CSO asked me to drive to the helipad. There were a few staff officers waiting for the Corps Commander. There was a helicopter waiting for the GOC, ready to take off. I was still thinking about the RR comn. I knew that to cover the vast corps sector, we had to have an innovative approach. We had to go for the heights. As I looked towards the East, I could see the skyline of hilltops just visible in the distant horizon lit up with a reddish glow by the morning sun.

"Those must be the Mizo hill ranges." I thought, "Aijal the capital of Mizoram must be somewhere beyond." I had earlier seen on my map that Aijal is about 4000 ft above MSL. From Aijal, the farthest point of the corps sector would not be more than 150 Km except perhaps for Dhaka and Cox's Bazar. From our Corps HQ location, it was around 80 km line-of-sight.

Suddenly I remembered my fleeting visit to the police radio detachment at Badarpur and the police operator telling me about the excellent comn with Aijal. It occurred to me, "Why not develop a *RR comn node* at Aijal with all its advantages of being secure and logistically sustainable?" That would mean moving 3 to 4 RR detachments to Aijal, 250 km away through long winding roads and hilly tracts; would take 3 days to reach. Once there, they would be on their own for the rest of the operations; a major RR comn node 100 km to the *East* divorced from the Corps sector; while the Corps thrust to Dhaka would be 150 to 200 km to the *West*. I knew this would be turned down as *most absurd*. But I felt that we should give this option a try. *(See notes 3 & 4)*

As we were waiting for the Corps Commander, I made myself bold to mention this idea to my CSO. Just then the Corps Commander arrived. My CSO just nodded and rushed to meet him. From a distance, I could see him articulating something to the GOC pointing towards the East. The CSO then called me. As I came near them, I heard the GOC telling my CSO, "Gurdyal, I am going to Badarpur; on my return I will be stopping over at Aijal for an hour. Ask Major Narayanan to hop in. He can plan the RR comn node at Aijal when we are there."

I had about an hour at Aijal. I interacted with Capt Pandey in charge of skeleton comn left behind after mobilisation for war. I gathered the following information from him in the short time that I had:

(i) Two brigades (61 & 73) of 57 Div were earlier deployed in Mizo Hills. On mobilisation a highly depleted 73 Brigade has been left behind at Aijal for the whole of Mizo Hills.

(ii) There is a single 10-line magneto exchange functioning and all the sig comns are through overhead PL and VHF radio using GPA (ground Plane Antenna).

(iii) They had earlier a single hop RR link from Aijal to Masimpur functioning very well. On mobilisation, all RR resources had been taken away.

My Own Assessment

Mizo Hills' ridges generally run from North to South; Aijal is a bowl located between two parallel ridges 5 to 10 km apart and could get clear RLOs path to Masimpur/Badarpur towards North through the ridge gap. Being a hilly terrain, any in-between low obstruction could be advantageous in giving 'obstacle gain'. This would be equally applicable for RR link from Aijal to Chittagong/Feni towards the South.

For single hop RR comn from Aijal to Teliamura (East to West), we may need to find a relatively higher location on the ridge. One possible location is PWD water tank area about 8 km away from the Army Exchange. But major advantages are that it is fenced all around and protected by DSC personnel. Mains power is available but with frequent shut downs, It has a roadable track for move of our vehicles. Another plus point was availability of Mains power. The location is relatively 750 ft higher from where we should be able to get a clear RLOS path to our location (Teliamura) to the West. See note (4).

I had noted down all the above relevant points for briefing my CO. I returned from Aijal late in the evening by helicopter and proceeded straight to my Regt HQ to brief my CO on my Aijal visit. My CO was initially furious that I had not consulted him before making any commitments to the CSO. But he very soon cooled down. I briefed him in detail on the Army setup and the skeleton signal resources left behind at Aijal. I also gave my own overall assessment and the positives of establishing a RR Node at Aijal.

My CO listened intently. He asked a very pointed question, "Does it mean that we cannot take Teliamura-Aijal RR link for granted and we need to carry out trials."

I answered, "Sir, I am confident the trials will be successful. It is worth the effort since both the operational sectors of 8 Div (Badarpur-Sylhet) in the North and 23 Div (Feni/Chittagaong) in the South will be fully covered as the operations progress. We should plan to send 3 or 4 RR terminals with generators, sufficient cables both field and carrier quad."

I continued, "I also suggest we carry one HF Radio terminal with RS C11/R210 for comn with us for our close monitoring and assistance till Aijal-Teliamura RR link is fully established."

My CO didn't say anything but appeared convinced. He immediately called on phone Capt Arjun Deva, a senior captain who was the RR officer,

> *"Arjun, I want you to establish an RR node at Aijal, resources permitting, with 3 or 4 RR terminals earliest. Do meet Maj Narayanan immediately for a detailed briefing. Thereafter, work out the resources required and be*

prepared to move as a convoy by morning 0900 hrs. tomorrow (8 September 71).

He now looked at me," Naru, you are already loaded with a lot of tasks and commitments. Do concentrate on these and leave the responsibility for establishing this crucial Aijal node to me. I will closely monitor and assist Arjun as required till the establishment of the node and Aijal-Teliamura RR link becomes functional."

I felt vindicated.

See Note (2) for Capt Arjun Deva's side of the Story; Notes (3) and (4) on RR comn ranges from Aijal and a few elementary RR comn range concepts.

POSTSCRIPT

My visit to Aijal was most timely and fruitful. The fact that I went with the Corps Commander had the desired effect. We got the full support of every unit/formation concerned. By mid Sep, we had established the RR comn node at Aijal fully. The Corps Terminal was on a high feature a few Km from the Army exchange in the PWD water tank area, fenced all around and had security guards from the DSC. It was an ideal site with no obstructions for RR comn. There was a lot of apprehension expressed initially on the success of this innovative initiative but all these stopped when the relay node started functioning. For the next three months, till the Corps HQ moved forward to *Comilla*, this RR node proved to be most effective in providing continuous and reliable RR comn to all the formation HQ when most needed.

NOTES

1 A word about a signal officer being referred to as "SPARROW". In the Radio Telephony (RT) procedure followed by the Army, appointment codes are used. E.g. TIGER is the code for the Comdr, LION for a G Staff officer and SPARROW for a Signal officer. These help in concealing the identity of the level of the , for example, TIGER refers to a comdr, be he a comdr of a Corps, Division (Div) or a Brigade (Bde). It has become a practice to call a signal officer a 'Sparrow'.

2 **Capt Arjun Deva's side of the story**

On 7 September 1971 late in the evening my CO tasked me to establish an RR node at Aijal, with 3 or 4 RR terminals earliest. He asked me to meet Maj Narayanan, our OC Engineering Company immediately who had just then returned from Aijal for a detailed briefing. He wanted me to assemble all the resources necessary and be ready and move as a convoy by the next day morning by 0800 hrs (08 September 71).

I rushed to the Regt HQ where Maj Narayanan was waiting. He described in detail on his visit to Aijal and his assessment of resources required and the tasks involved for establishment of RR node at Aijal. We thereafter worked out the specialist and GS vehicles and other essential resources required. I returned to the RR Hill and without wasting time I commenced the activities related to our convoy move the next day morning.

Our convoy consisted of four RR vehicles with generators, one HF Radio vehicle (RS C11/R210) and two GS vehicles, one for carrying Carrier Quad (CQ), and field cable and two full-fledged tents and the second for Adm/Recce Support. I assembled the det personnel and briefed them about the assignment. Through the night, I got the vehicles and the equipment checked for serviceability and road worthiness. Altogether, there were seven 1-Ton vehicles and these were kept ready for move to Aijal the next day.

On 8 Sept, around 08.00 hrs after having early breakfast and packed lunch, I marched the convoy of seven vehicles with two generators and two trailers after approval from my CO.

We had night stopover at Masimpur (8/9 Sept night). We started for Aijal in the morning around 0900 hrs. Initially the road was good but as we entered Mizo hilly region, it became treacherous with long winding tracks road bends. I ensured that movement of our convoy of five vehicles was slow never exceeding 30 Kmph. We reached Aijal safely around 1630 hrs (9 Sept) at the Line Detachment (Det) location left behind by 57 Mtn Div. The officer in-charge Lt PK Singh showed the RR area about 50m away from where the earlier RR terminal was working with Masimpur. It was getting dark as also raining, One Det earmarked for providing link to Masimpur was left at the RR area to be kept ready by 2000 hrs. (9 Sep).

For RR comn to Teliamura, I first wanted to see the location of PWD water tank area and hence proceeded there with the other RR Det comdr. We noticed that this area was partially accessible, but secure with landline communication and had commercial power supply. Since the area was under Border Road (Pushpak), I had to get their approval. Fortunately, Capt SN Pandey sparrow of Pushpak Project of the Border Road

Organisation (BRO) happened to be my course mate at the IMA. He spoke to the authorities concerned on my behalf and directed the Security Staff to permit us to establish RR terminal at the site We moved the RR terminal earmarked for Aijal-Teliamura (Corps HQ) link, and other administrative vehicles by 2300 hrs near the site, the equipment and the antenna masts were dismounted and manually brought to the water tank cabin. Generator was sited. By then it was past midnight around 0130 hrs (10 Sept). I was keen to establish the RR link to Teliamura at the earliest. It was dark and there was heavy chilly wind blowing across. Fortunately, my det personnel were highly motivated.

The water tank area was on a slope with hardly any flat piece of ground sufficient to anchor mast ropes. It was a stupendous effort to erect two antenna masts one for Transmit and the other for receive. We managed to get to a mast height of 44 ft as against a maximum of 48 ft by 0300 hrs (10 Sept). We switched in the sets around 0330 hrs. Our Corps terminal at Teliamura had been on listening watch since evening. Our receiver monitor showed some deflection. We felt there was some hope. Soon, after further tuning, the monitor deflection improved and I could speak to my radio mechanic at Teliamura end on the audio channel. Thereafter normal procedures were followed at either end to optimise the signal strength with further antenna alignment. When we got a near full scale deflection (FSD), the carrier equipment ACT (1+4)3A was connected. I tested all the 4 carrier channels. I got one channel extended to our Corps exchange at Teliamura and asked the operator for my CO. It was around 0430 hrs on 10 Sept. My CO came up on the line. He was expecting the call.

"Sir, Arjun here from the location at Aijal; we are through to you on all the four channels. Two Channels will be extended on RR directly to the Masimpur exchange by soonest today evening (10 Sept); we have to lay carrier quad cable from the exchange to this Det location involving 8 to 9 kms laying distance. My CO replied, "Well done. Do convey my congratulations to your det personnel. Don't forget to inform Maj Narayanan. Brief me in detail tomorrow after fully establishing the RR node." I informed Maj Narayanan accordingly.

I later briefed my CO and Maj Narayanan in the evening around 1800 hrs on establishment of direct RR link from Teliamura to Masimpur through the Aijal RR node with two Carrier speech channels extended directly between Teliamura and Masimpur

I took next seven to eight days to fully establish the RR node after resolving all administrative and logistics issues.

3 **Radio Relay Comn Ranges from AIJAL**

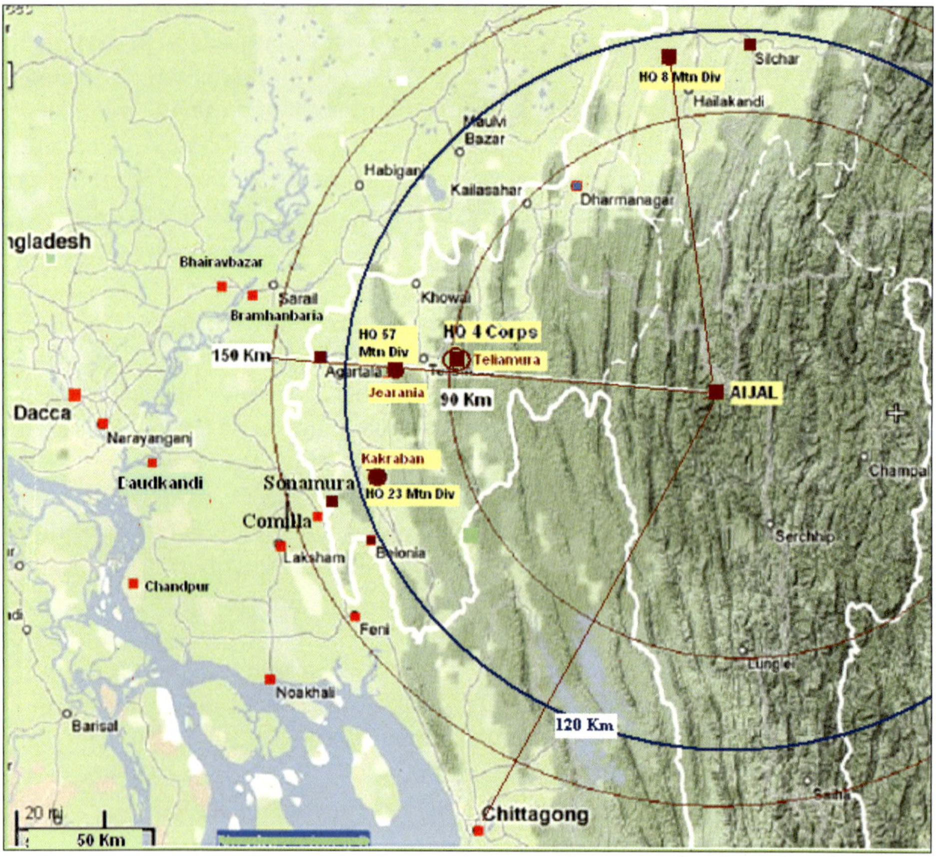

Courtesy Google Map

Based on the operational tasks given to IV Corps viz. destroying Pak forces East of River Meghna and occupy Comilla, Chandpur, Feni and Chittagong, we had to plan the comn anticipating the likely move of all the formation HQ. Our major concern was the **Badarpur–Sylhet axis** in the North and **Feni-Chittagong axis in the South**. The RR Node at Aijal could practically cover these two axes to reach any formation HQ moving within 120 to 130 Km radius thus effectively cover the projected Operational sector.

4 **A note on RR comn ranges:**

Line of sight (LOS) is the direct free-space path that exists between two points. Using binoculars on a clear day, it is easy to determine if visual line of sight exists between two points that are separated miles apart. To have a clear line of sight there must be no obstructions between the two locations.

Radio transmission requires a clear path between antennas known as Radio

Line of Sight (RLOS); a term used for radio surface comn ranges. Radio waves tend to bend round the earth's curvature due to refraction and hence RLOS is generally greater than LOS.

Our Radio Relay Stations were based on RS C41/R222, British vintage equipment of the late 60s and early 70s; these were crystal controlled in the frequency band 50 to 100 MHz. The transmitter C41 and Receiver R222 needed separate frequency for duplex working.

RR directional antenna (YAGI) with a mast height at 36 ft at both ends, gave LOS distance of 25 km. We always tried to use maximum mast height of 48 ft and tried to locate them on mounds or small hillocks with relative heights of 50 to 100 ft wherever possible.

Aijal with its height of 4300 ft gave ranges of 120-150 Km with our C41/R222 sets. As a relay node Aijal was ideal from all considerations viz. physical security, technical & logistical.

I have avoided technical jargons like Fresno Zone (FZ) and FFZ clearance. For those interested, I recommend:

http://www.fab-corp.com/pages.php?pageid=2 http://www.terabeam.com/support/calculations/fresnel-zone.php

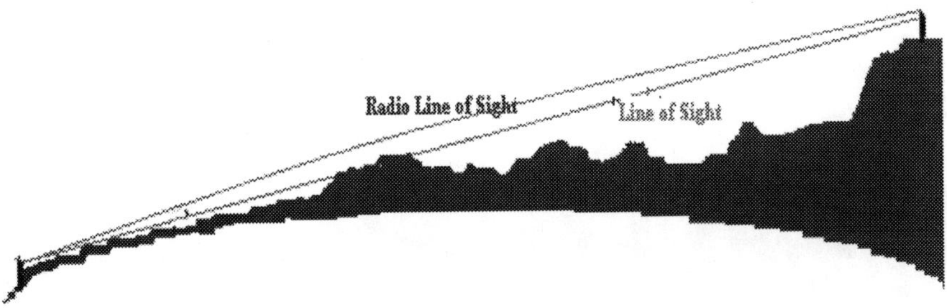

- Line of Sight – LOS Obstructed
- Radio LOS (curved path) – clears the obstruction

PART II

Signal Comn for Headquarters IV Corps: 15 Sep to 16 Dec 1971

Signal comn is a force multiplier to win battles and ultimately the war. When timely, it can prevent unwanted battles and save human lives and war resources.

6

Signal Comn build up at Teliamura: 15 Sep to 06 Dec 1971

By mid Sep 1971, the Corps HQ and our Regiment had moved to the new location; a beautiful undulating land with tender bamboo growth all around. The office and work place were all based on bamboo cottages called *'bashas'* expertly made by the local bamboo workers. In our tents, we had bamboo cots and tables all done by these locals, in exchange for *a meal and a tot of rum* from the *langar (soldier's kitchen).*

In the initial few days, frogs and snakes were often spotted in our toilet tent. On one occasion, a snake, perfectly coiled up, was having its afternoon siesta under my cot. On being disturbed, it quietly slipped out and disappeared in the bamboo bushes outside. I was told that these snakes were non-poisonous and harmless. With large-scale human movements, the snakes disappeared. The weather during the day started to improve, nights were always pleasant, and the monsoon rains had also slowly receded. Because of the nature of the undulations and the bamboo undergrowth, we had to leave our jeeps in convenient car parks nearer the tracks. We had to walk a lot but started enjoying the same. That also made us very fit.

By early Oct 71, our comn had been established as per scale and fully stabilised. Our carrier center housing both army and the P&T equipment was housed in a sturdy shed made of CGI sheets. We had sited it in a cutout carved out of the side of a mound. The engineers had provided shellproof overhead protection (OHP) with sandbags riveting.

During the preparatory phase of the operations in Sep and early

Oct, *Radio Silence* had been imposed. We had located the radio village in a large bowl formed by the undulations of the land, very close to the Signal Centre and the Exchange. The medium power radio vehicles, all Siemen's 400 Watts were well dispersed and positioned in dugouts, neatly camouflaged. These dug outs were expertly made by our Engineers with dozers with convenient entry and exit slopes. We did not put up the *'triple folded dipole aerials'* to avoid detection from air. But we had positioned the mast bases and the sections that could be erected readily with ease. Since the *radio silence* was imposed, during the night as part of *detachment (det) drills*, the Det Personnel *erected and dismantled the dipole aerials*, went through the tuning procedure of the *Siemen's 400 Watt* sets without switching on the power. We had also extended the remote control lines for radio speech channels to the exchange and the *Ops Room*.

On 14 Oct night around 11.00 pm, my CO called me to say that the *'Radio Silence'* had been lifted and wanted the corps radio links to be activated immediately. We were ready for this and by 3.00 am, early morning, we had established as many as six medium power radio links with their *triple folded dipole aerials* and had taken the test calls through the remote-control lines. *Lt Tarun Mahendra* was in the Ops Room vehicle from 3.00 am onwards, taking test calls and assisting the Staff Officers on duty with their Radio Telephony (RT) calls.

The RR village was located about two-km away on an elevated piece of land without any obstructions to gain height and comn ranges. We had dug outs with suitable OHP for all the RR terminals against enemy shelling and bombing.

We had grouped one RR terminal with each formation. Normally a Havildar or a Naik commands a RR detachment. However, for the RR terminals grouped with the formations, I had attached an officer or a JCO for better coordination and response. This was also in line with my CSO's directions to put best efforts at the *other end*. This decision proved to be most effective later during fast fluid operations when the formation HQ moved frequently.

The RR node at *Aijal* proved very effective. We had two formations under the Corps (8 and 23 Div) linked to the Corps HQ at Teliamura through the Aijal node. In addition, we had catered for one additional formation (fmn) HQ coming directly under the Corps during the offensive phase of the operations. This was indeed a bold and most unconventional approach in that fmn HQ was free to move anywhere in the sector and simply *hook on** to the Aijal node as long as they were within the RR comn range.

We were also fully aware that once the formation HQ crossed the IB, our RR comn from Aijal would become marginal. I had, therefore, planned a RR Node at Sonamura much similar to the Aijal node. But we didn't have spare RR terminals, as all that we had were fully committed on ground. Around early November, we received 8 RR terminals from B Corps Signal Regt under new raising at Tezpur in support of our Corps. With these, we could establish the Sonamura node. Also, we could afford to group an additional terminal with each of the two formations HQ (23 and 57 Div) who would be within RR range from *Sonamura node*. By this, we could cater to both the Main and Tac HQ of these two formations to be in contact with the Corps HQ. *See Sketch Map and Notes thereto on the next page.*

Immediately after the War, I wrote an article: *'Reminiscences'* in April 1972 in **'Signalman'** (*See Appendix* 2). This will give an idea of the positive state of signal comn by Oct 71.

IV Corps Sector: RR, PL and Microwave (P&T) Comn (15 Sep – 3 Dec 1971)

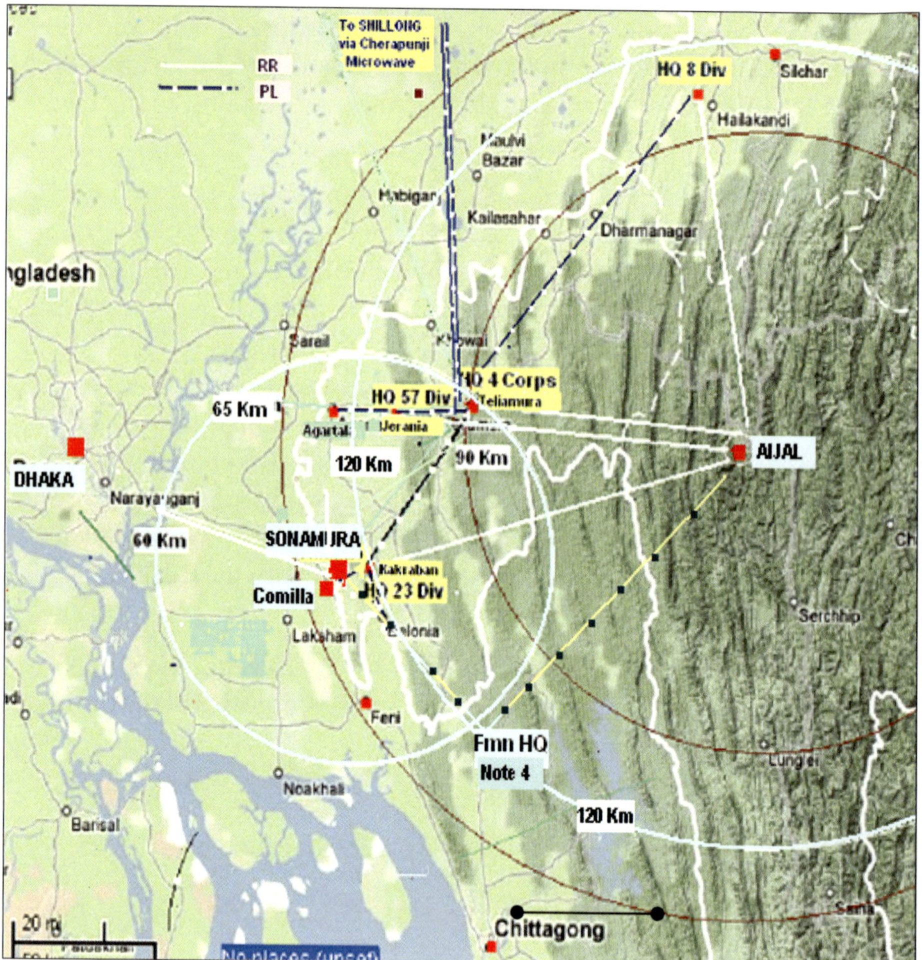

50 km *Courtesy: Google Map*

Notes:

1. **Microwave**: Teliamura to Shillong with a repeater at Cherapunji by the P&T to provide the requisite Speech and telegraph (VFT) circuits as no landline connectivity was possible.
2. **PL**: Only the connectivity shown. Not the actual route.
3. **RR**:
   - *HQ 8 Mtn Div:* RR with even two relays to Badarpur/Patherkandi was not feasible. We had to choose Aijal to give the height advantage. From Aijal, we could get ranges of 120-130 Km depending upon the location. (Shown in white circle)

- *HQ 57 Mtn Div:* There was really no signal comn problem to Jerania; yet we had made provision for RR connectivity to Aijal node for the offensive phase.
- *HQ 23 Mtn Div:* RR (single hop) to Kakraban was marginal. We also had to plan for the offensive phase considering that one of the 23 Div op tasks was to capture Chitagong. Aijal node could support move of HQ 23 Div on the Feni-Chitagong axis.

4 **Limited Grid**:

Sonamura RR Node: Towards the West, we had planned RR node at Sonamura, which could easily cover the Meghna River line (Brahman baria-Daudkandi-Chandpur With the height advantage at both Teliamura RR Hill and Sonamura, we could get single hop range of 70 Km. We had also planned RR ranges of 60 Km from Sonamura; and in conjunction with the Aijal node, we had also planned a limited grid for the formations moving on the **Feni-Chittagong** axis. (See Sketch)

Note:

Dhaka the capital of E Pakistan was never in the scheme of things even as late as 1 Dec 71. As it later turned out, we had to establish a Relay at Daudkandi for comn to Dhaka from Comilla where the Corps HQ moved on 11 Dec after the fall of Comilla.

7

Radio Relay link to Tactical HQ 23 Infantry Division on Night: 6/7 Dec 1971

"How does the God accede to the prayers of people in crisis? Surely He must be fulfilling this through ordinary people inspiring them to perform tasks beyond their call of duty or limits of human endurance or both."

IV Corps offensive commenced on 3 Dec 71 and by 9/10 Dec, the leading formations of 23 and 57 Divisions had secured important towns and comn centers viz. Akhaura, Brahmanbaria, Bhairav-bazar, Comilla and *Laksham*; In fact the leading elements had reached three key points on Meghna, i.e. Ashuganj, Daudkandi and Chandpur as early as 5 Dec and secured the East Bank of River Meghna by 9 Dec thus opening up the approaches to Dhaka.

In the North, 8 Division had cleared Maulvi-bazar, secured Sherpur/ Shadipur ferry site and had surrounded Sylhet, and the siege was later to continue till 17 Dec when the Sylhet garrison surrendered. The operations were fast and swift.

We were fully aware that the forward comn links would deteriorate when the formation HQ cross the IB and move beyond *120 Km aerial distance from Aijal. (See sketch)*. We had therefore planned a relay node on a small-elevated piece of land at *Sonamura overlooking Comilla* across the border. I was confident that with the height advantage, we would get RR range of 60 to 65 km for control of the operations beyond *Comilla-Laksham* and up-to the River *Meghna line*.

I now wish to narrate an incident on the night 6/7 Dec 1971 *during the War*. This I had covered in my article Reminiscences in *"The Signalman"* written just after the War (See Appendix 2). Due to the page restrictions, I could not tell the whole story that time.

One of the formations was 23 Division. The Division HQ was all along located at *Kakraban* about 80 km Southwest of *Teliamura* and close to *Sonamura*. It was imminent for the HQ to move forward and our RR terminal grouped with them was expected to move at any time. I had attached a smart young JCO *Naib Subedar Nasib Singh* with this detachment. I had briefed him about the Sonamura RR Node and that he should hook up with this node from the new location. On 6 Dec during the day, the Main HQ 23 Div moved in the general area towards SW of *Comilla*. Actual location was *Village Buschi* about 14 km short of *Laksham* a strong hold of the enemy with a brigade group.

Around 4 pm, *Subedar Dinkar Natu*, in charge RR node at *Sonamura* spoke to me; I was at the RR Hill at Teliamura. (Corps HQ end). The speech was too faint. He had walked down 3 km to the Public Call Office (PCO) to make the call as there was no line comn to the RR node. Here is a gist of the message conveyed:

1. Main HQ 23 Div RR has not opened up as yet. He is waiting for the RR signals. As regards the rear RR link to the Corps HQ, his Transmit Frequency Crystal was faulty and hence he is not able to tune the Transmitter. A new set of crystals was urgently required.
2. There was only one generator. For 24-hour operation, a second generator was needed along with sufficient diesel.

I immediately called and briefed *Capt Nirmal Dhillon*, my Officer in Charge RR. Nirmal was a bright officer who had recently joined us after attending a course on Radio Relay at *MCTE Mhow*. I was confident that he would attend to the requirements. I became extremely busy thereafter attending to a number of other priority comn tasks.

Around 11 pm, I suddenly remembered about the RR link to Tac HQ. Although it was late in the night, I decided to go to the RR Hill. It was pitch dark there. I located the Tac HQ RR 'dug out'.

When I entered, I saw *Capt Nirmal* inside. He appeared to be nervous. The link was not through. It was obvious that our vehicle and the generator trailer had not reached. I was deeply worried about the frequency crystals, without which comn was just not possible.

I knew that the Corps Commander always talked to the Divisional Commander early in the morning and we had to get this RR link 'through' at any cost. Just then there was a ring. It was *Subedar Natu*. He was speaking on a line extended to the Relay location by Major J M Khullar of the Comn Zone Signal Regiment. The line was noisy and speech too faint and unfit for normal comn.

"Naru Sir, can you hear me?" It was Jimmy Khullar my SODE18 course mate, "Sub Natu wants to talk to you urgently."

I just couldn't believe what was happening. I heaved a sigh of relief. It was indeed a *divine intervention* through *Jimmy Khullar.*

Sub Natu came up on the line:

"Sir, I met Maj Khullar Sahib by chance at the PCO. The PCO line is faulty. I mentioned to him that I have to contact you urgently. He immediately got his line party on the PL route to extend a temporary line using field cable to this Relay location. They had to lay close to 3 Km of field cable; hence the delay in contacting you; But for Khullar Sahib, I couldn't have spoken to you."

I profusely thanked Jimmy for the timely help. Jimmy, typical of him, responded thus; "Naru Sir, you are my Guru. If I can't do this for you, for whom else will I do?"

Sub Natu confirmed that the vehicle had reached an hour back. The delay was due to the vehicle breaking down enroute. He also added hesitantly that the new frequency crystal that we had sent was seriously getting interference from the forward RR link.

The time was 1130 pm night 6 Dec. I had to ensure that a new set of frequency crystals fully compatible reaches Sonamura before 0400 am to give him enough time to put through the RR link in time for the Corps Commander's call.

What follows is an account of the happenings on that eventful night 6/7 Dec 1971 between 1130 pm and 0430 am.

Sketch: HQ IV Corps to Tactical HQ 23 Inf Div: Radio Relay link Night 6/7 Dec 71

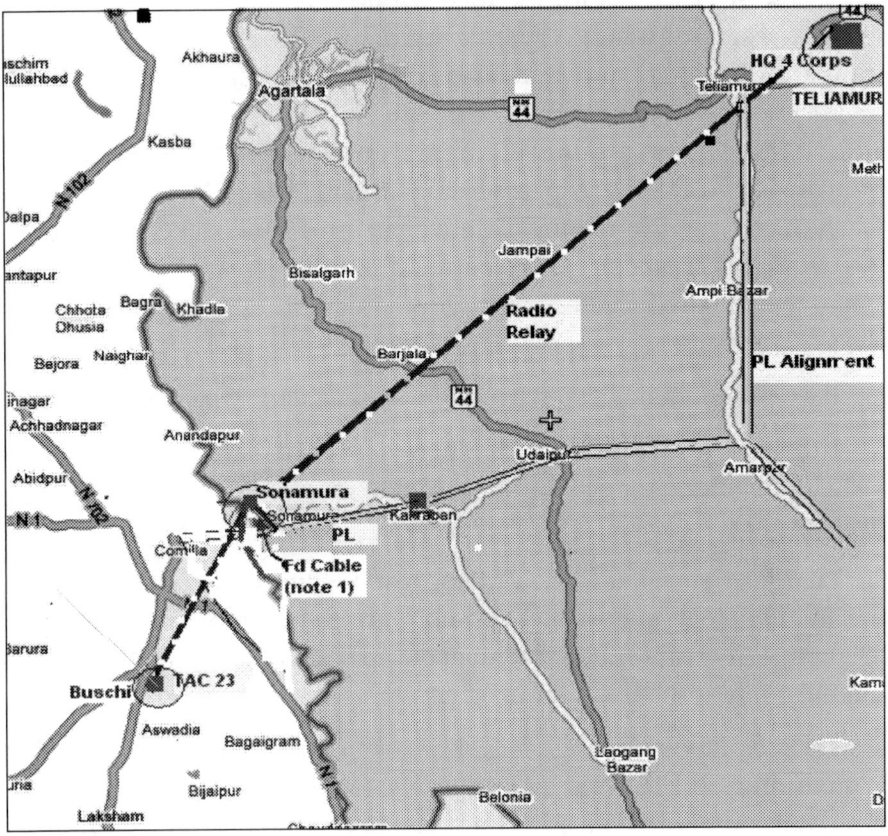

←20 Km→ *Courtesy Google Map*

Note 1: Field cable extended by Maj Khullar

Tac HQ 23 Div (Buschi)	Relay (Sonamura)	Teliamura (HQ IV Corps)
(Nb Sub Saini)	(Nb Sub Natu)	(Maj Narayanan/Capt Dhillon)

06 Dec 71 **1630 hrs Capt** *Dhillon sends Single RR terminal with a generator (and Freq Crystal to Relay location (Sonamura)*

2200 hrs *Maj Malay Ghosh (SO2 Sigs) at Buschi. Ensures Tac 23 RR is open.*

2300 hrs *Maj Narayanan at the RR hill. Gets a call from Maj Khullar/Nb Sub Natu.*

2330 hrs *Sigmn Barkat Ram Driver proceeds to Sonamura with the New Freq Crystal*

07 Dec 71 **0330 hrs** *Barkat Ram reaches Sonamura (80 Km drive in the night)*

0415 hrs *GOC's call put through to the 23 Div Comdr.*

Note: Our Radio Relay Stations were based on RS C41 / R222, British vintage equipment of the late 60s and early 70s;these were crystal controlled in the frequency band 50 to 100 MHz. The transmitter C41 and Receiver R222 needed separate frequency (piezo electric) crystals for the operating frequency stability; this is unlike the modern radio equipment, which is based on frequency synthesizers.

1130 pm to midnight

I ascertain from Sub Natu the forward link frequencies. Capt Nirmal reviews the frequency crystals held by us, refers to frequency compatibility chart and manages to select one new set. I pass the frequency information to Subedar Natu so that he has enough time to adjust the Yagi Antenna elements suiting the new frequency. Concurrently, I call my jeep driver-Signalman Barkat Ram. Briefed him that he has to go to Sonamura to deliver an important packet (containing the frequency crystals), get his petrol tank full and carry an extra jerry can. I also ensured that a vehicle mechanic with essential spares and tools accompanies.

Barkat Ram in my jeep with a vehicle mechanic was ready to leave.

I distinctly recall that moment when I was standing before an ordinary soldier trying to motivate him to realise the importance of the mission.

"Barkat Ram, you have a major responsibility. You have to reach the frequency crystal packet to Sub Natu Sahib at Sonamura before 0330 a.m. Drive carefully. Remember our unit's reputation and our Corps (Signals) image is now in your hands".

I called Naik Jagir Singh at Kakraban and briefed him about Barkat Ram coming with the frequency crystals; asked him to wait on the Main Road and on his arrival, escort his jeep to the RR node at Sonamura. I kept walking around anxiously in pitch darkness around the RR village, all the time praying for Barkat Ram's safe journey to Sonamura. The time was 0315 am.

Here is a sequence of events over the next 90 minutes till 0430 am:

0315 am

Naik Jagir Singh calls from Kakraban.

"Sir, Barkat Ram has just reached our location. I rushed just to inform you. The road to Sonamura is good; we should reach there in the next 30 minutes." I feel greatly relieved.

0345 am

We are glued to our RR terminal with the transmitter and receiver 'ON';

we are looking at the receiver signal strength meter. The pointer is showing 'Zero' indicating "NO signal."

0400 am

The pointer suddenly swings to near full-scale deflection.

Sub Natu's voice comes up clear on the speaker, "Sir, we are through to Tac HQ. I shall tune up and patch the channel to Tac HQ in the next 10 minutes."

0415 am

I speak to Subedar Nasib Singh at the Tac HQ on RR. Just then, we get a call from our Exchange to enquire if we are through to Tac HQ, as the Corps Commander wants to speak to the Div Comdr.

0420 am

The call is connected. The Div Comdr comes up on the line first as per protocol. The exchange operator is connecting to the Corps Commander. I am extremely tired and sleepy. I have my headphones. Although unethical, like any eager signal officer, my only concern at that time was whether the speech quality is good.

Suddenly, I hear the Corps Commander (Gen Sagat Singh), and I listen to the entire conversation.

Corps Comdr: "Hira, can you hear me? What's happening?'

Div Comdr (Maj Gen Hira): "Sir, All well. I have a surprise for you."

CC: "What Surprise?"

DC: We are poised for an attack on that xxxxx garrison. The pre-dawn attack is being launched in the next 45 minutes."

CC: "I have seen the entire sector yesterday from my helicopter. Paks are in disarray. Why suffer avoidable casualties at this stage? Pound the position with your artillery. They are already softened with our air strikes yesterday. They will surrender soon."

DC: "Sir, do you want me to call off the operation?"

CC: "I leave the decision to you.

DC: "Right Sir.

The call is over. Due to sheer exhaustion and lack of sleep, I must have dozed off for a few minutes. My radio mechanic wakes me up, "Sir, have some Tea." I look at my watch. It shows 04.30 am. I am in a trance, unsure of whether the conversation that I heard on RR just a few minutes back was real or merely my dream?

POSTSCRIPT

I honestly never bothered to find out which that operation was and whether it was actually called off. It was only recently in 2006 over the web site, I chanced to read in the War History 1971 about the 23 Div operations relating to the capture of *Lakṣham town*; that by first light 6 Dec 1971, the town was isolated from North and West. It was strongly defended by a brigade group. Hence it was not attacked on 6 or 7 Dec 1971, but was subjected to intensive air strikes and artillery fire. As appreciated by the Corps Comdr, much of the enemy had vacated and by 8/9 Dec the town was secured with minimum casualty. *(1)*

All the same, I have been carrying the memories of that night 6/7 Dec 1971 for three decades and a half; and had always believed that a major offensive operation on an enemy stronghold was averted by timely signal comn by us the IV Corps Signals. I am now past 74 (2008) and as I recall those events now after 37 years, philosophically, I cannot help wondering:

"How does the God accede to the prayers of people in crisis? Surely he must be fulfilling this through ordinary people inspiring them to perform tasks beyond their call of duty or limits of human endurance or both."

How else can I explain as to why I decided suddenly on that night of 6/7 Dec 1971 to go to the RR hill? Why Major Khullar from nowhere extended a telephone line to my RR node at Sonamura? How an ordinary soldier driver Barkat Ram drove that night over 80 Km carrying the essential frequency crystal without any mishap and reached Sonamura just in time? Why the Corps Comdr spoke to the Div Comdr in that early morning hours and suggested to the Div Comdr to call off the planned attack?"

Over the years, I have asked myself several times, "Was a major battle really averted?

If so, "Who were those saved? Who all were from the enemy and who from own troops? How many of them were fathers of young children; sons of old parents, husbands of long separated wives, brothers, friends, fiancées?" I have no idea; but I do know that everyone among them would have been praying for an early end to the War, safe return and reunion with their close and loved ones.

I am proud of those officers, JCOs and other ranks from the Corps of Signals who were associated with me on that night; every one of them performed tasks beyond their call of duty in the best traditions of the Corps. *"The God perhaps,* ***did smile*** *through them!"*

I have over years tried to find an answer to these questions: -

What is it that motivates only a few to perform beyond their call of duty?

Why only some go out of the way to help others?"

The incident on that night on 6/7 Dec 1971 and further reaffirmed by many such events later in my lifetime has given me this answer:

"Surely, that must be for the God to **smile** more often."

NOTE

1. **Capture of Laksham**

   ... ... At this stage it was discovered that Laksham Complex was well defended by about a brigade group and hence it was decided not to attack it. Instead it was subjected to intense air strikes and artillery shelling from 6 Dec onwards. As on 7 Dec reports were received that Baghmera (RR 2877) situated at the southern part of Lalmai Hills, had been vacated by the Pak troops. ... ... The bulk of the Pak troops had abandoned Laksham town on the night of 8/9 Dec, leaving behind huge quantities of arms and ammunition. ... ...

Extract from Official *"War History 1971"* MoD Govt of India,
Ch 13: March to Dhaka, p. 552

Maj M K Ghosh's (SO2 Signals) side of the Story:

RR link to 23 Div HQ - 7 to 9 Dec 1971

On 6 Dec the CSO called me in the afternoon and asked me to go forward towards 23 Div Loc and find out why the rear link from their side had not yet been put through .He told me that he was worried because the Div had not been in comn ever since they kicked off on their advance. I accordingly started for Kakraban. On reaching there, I found nobody, but could see the ARROW Signs put up by the MPs marking the Centre Line of their advance. I followed these arrows along a village track till I reached a wide metalled Highway. Near the junction of the track and the highway a milestone indicated that this was the Dhaka-Chittagong highway. There was a Provo det of 23 Div at this junction who stopped us till some more vehicles, all replenishment and B echelon trucks, joined up. It was dark by then. We were allowed to move forward as a convoy escorted by two Armored cars. This convoy led us to Buschi village where the Div HQ was located. The time was around 2030 hrs. I found my way to the signal centre where I met the CO 23 Div Sig Regt. He told me that they did not even try to open the Rear link on RR on orders from the Divisional Commander (Div Cdr). I conveyed the CSO's message to him and he instructed the OC 1 Company (Coy) to put through the link soonest.

I thereafter retired to the Officers mess and tried to sleep on a tabletop. But there was to be no sleep as the Enemy had an Artillery Battery at Laksham (Incidentally the Div loc was not beyond Laksham but about 12 to 14 Kms short of it within Arty fire range), which started shelling our own Medium Artillery Regt gun area and the wagon lines. A fire started when an ammunition dump in the wagon lines was hit. The CO of the Arty Regt died while trying to supervise rescue operations in the wagon lines area.

The next day i.e. 7 Dec early morning, I was informed that the RR (Main HQ 23 Div to Corps) was through. On speaking to the CSO and informing him of the situation, He asked me to return but try to come back through Camilla as he had heard that Comilla town had been liberated. I started back accordingly and took the Chittagong - Dhaka road back towards Comilla.

Enroute I passed through many villages where I saw 'Jai Bangla' Torans (Decorated gateways) being erected and my vehicle was welcomed and waved forward with shouts of 'Jai Bangla'. Some of the culverts and Small bridges had been damaged but our sappers (engineers) had made them passable by single vehicles; reached Comilla just before noon. The locals had started celebrating. I found my way to the civil exchange by asking the locals. At the Exchange location I found trenches and weapon pits, which appeared to have been vacated recently. The office and residential quarters of the DET Mr. Shaukat Usman were located within the Telephone Exchange premises. I asked for the DET who appeared a little later.

He welcomed me telling me that mine was the first Indian Military vehicle that he had encountered and that everyone was happy that the Pakistanis had fled. He stated that the Exchange was guarded by a platoon from The Pak Army till the early hours of that morning after which they vacated and presumably had gone to MYNAMATI Cantt where a Pak Brigade was located. He then showed me around the Exchange which was a Siemens Auto exchange of 100 lines capacity along with a number of Assistance and Trunk positions, which were fully functioning and manned. He then accompanied me to the circuit house premises, which was large and according to him had an extensive UG cable layout allowing for connectivity to a large number of telephones, if required. It occurred to me that the circuit house could be a good location for the Corps HQ when it moves up to Comilla. I collected a number of blueprints from the DET showing the UG cable layout extended around the Town. Incidentally the trunk circuits to Dhaka, Chittagong as also the junction line to the Pak Brigade exchange at Mynamati were working though those places were in Pakistani hands.

Thereafter, I returned to Teliamura via Belonia border after some adventures which included visiting the Police comn centre and confiscating he Crystals from the VHF/UHF radios through which they were communicating even then with Dhaka, Chittagong and other places. The Policemen were all Punjabi Muslims and rather unfriendly. At Belonia I found an Engineers det clearing mines followed by a signals det from N comn Z Signal Regt who were connecting the PL route constructed from Teliamura by their Regiment to the Epic route to Comilla thus establishing a direct PL connectivity to Comilla.

Late in the evening around 9 pm (7 Dec), I reached the Corps HQ and went straight to the CSO where I briefed him about the Telecom facilities and all that I had seen at Comilla.

The next day (8 Dec) the CSO went to Comilla accompanied by Maj K P S Gill of HQ Eastern Command Signals who had brought the much-needed Radio relay crystals, finally, the previous day. They met Mr. Usman there and did their own recce there.

(continued as Additional note of Chapter 8)

8

Move to and Signal Comn from Comilla: 11/12 Dec 1971

"... I don't think there is any parallel in History where a Corps Headquarters moved within enemy gun shells as we moved into COMILLA. And we couldn't possibly have moved there, unless Brigadier SIDHU and his Corps of Signals had ensured our comn. Now this is something, Ladies and Gentlemen, a fact of history and undeniable. The whole Corps Headquarters moved on the night of 11/12 Dec (1971) and we couldn't have functioned there, if we had not gone ahead and established the comn within enemy gun range...."

—GOC IV Corps on Signals Anniversary at Tezpur 15 Feb 72

The break out by the IV Corps formations and pursuit to Dhaka were fast and rapid. A few formations under our Corps who had crossed the IB on 2/3 Dec, advanced towards River Meghna and by 5 Dec, the troops had reached three key points on *Meghna R, i.e. Ashuganj, Daudkandi and Chandpur* opening up the approaches to *Dhaka*. By 9/10 Dec, many of them had crossed or were in the process of crossing Meghna on way to Dhaka. The operations were fast and swift. *Please see Sketch Map.*

It became clear that Main IV Corps HQ had to move forward from Teliamura either to Agartala or cross the IB and go to Comilla in E Pakistan. Agartala being in own territory and right on the IB, had all the advantages of easy build up and secure rear comn to higher formation HQ at Calcutta and Delhi. However, forward RR comn ranges would be stretched when the formations go beyond *Meghna* and *Padma* rivers on way to Dhaka. The second option was going to Comilla: but the problem was the rear comn to Calcutta and Delhi.

We had positioned the *"Systems Vehicle"* along with the RR node at Sonamura. *Hav Jadhav*, an expert with the P&T type of Carrier and VFT equipment was its in charge. By this, we had the flexibility to move this specialist vehicle at short notice either to Agartala or Comilla depending upon where the Corps HQ moved. (See sketch map).

We had always known that the logical location for the next move of the Corps HQ was *Comilla*; from where single hop RR would easily cover up to the *Meghna River line*; and with a relay station at *Daudkandi* could reach beyond Dhaka.

Signal Comn Build up for Move to Comilla: Night 10/11 Dec 1971

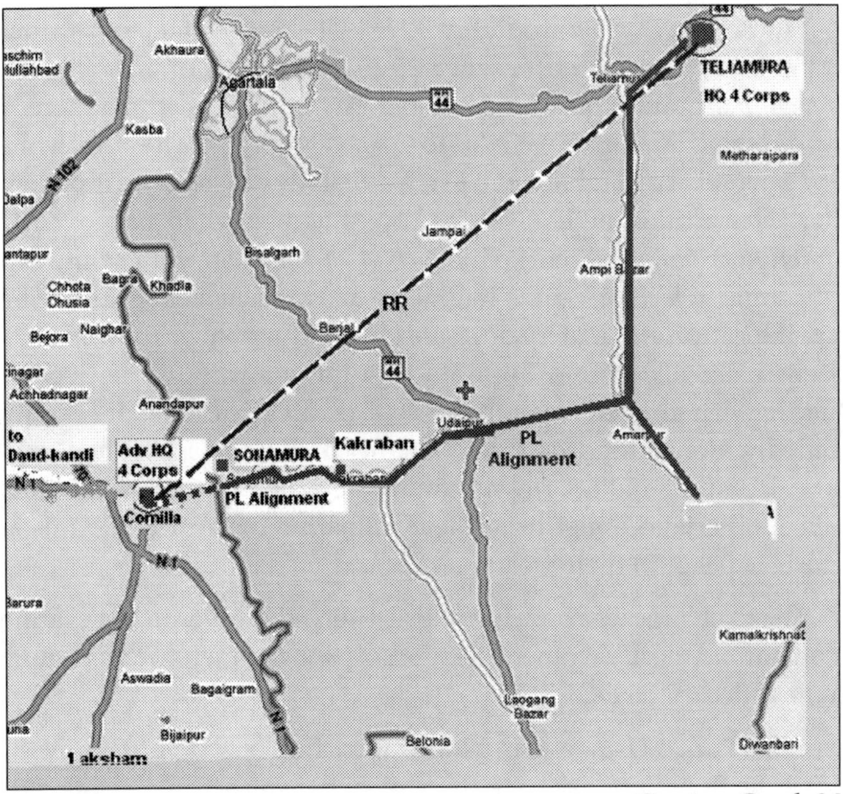

←20 km→ *Courtesy Google Map*

On 7 and 8 Dec, Malay Ghosh (SO2 Signals) and the CSO had gone to Comilla and had liaised with Mr. *Shaukat Usman*, Divisional Engineer Telephones (DET) Comilla. *(1)*. Malay called me late in the night of 8 Dec that I was to meet him first thing in the morning the next day (9 Dec) and thereafter be prepared to go to Comilla. The CSO perhaps wanted to make sure that there would be no implementation problems.

On 9 Dec mornings, Malay briefed me. I also saw the CSO. My brief was *to examine*:

- The feasibility of extending rearward comn from Comilla to our higher formations at Shillong, Calcutta, Delhi etc. through our Corps Carrier Center at Teliamura;
- Whether the exchange at Comilla can be made use of, if the Corps HQ moved there?

I started for *Comilla* around 10:00 am. The road distance was around 90 km to *Sonamura* and another 25 to 30 km to Comilla. I reached *Sonamura* around 1 pm. *Sub Natu and Hav Jadhav* joined me there. We crossed the IB and took the road to *Comilla* Highway. The stretch of the road beyond the IB for about 8 Km was bad due to long years of disuse after the partition in 1947. Our Corps Engineers had improved this stretch and had also marked *a portion* of the road with white tapes indicating *"vehicle safe lane."* Engineers had breached enemy mine field in that location and had made a safe lane for the vehicle movement. We reached *Comilla* around 3 pm and found our way to the Exchange Building. There were curious spectators, all local Bengalis shouting excitedly, "Joi Bangla" meaning "Victory to Bangladesh". They treated us with respect and courtesy. I could sense their feelings; liberation of their motherland, relief from the domination of West Pakistanis and return of peace in their area.

The Exchange was buzzing with activity; there were a large number of operators (mostly women), technicians and linemen. We were guided to the office of the DET.

Mr. Shaukat Usman was middle aged and looked very impressive. He spoke fluent English with the typical Bengali accent. He offered us tea and some snacks. We felt homely.

It was obvious that the CSO and Malay Ghosh had briefed him on what we wanted. The meeting lasted for about 45 minutes. He reiterated what was discussed and promised the following:

- The complete Exchange both the Trunk and the Local along with the operators and other essential staff would be at our disposal;
- He, in his capacity as DET, would accordingly function and report to the CSO or his designated staff.
- As directed by the CSO, construction/rehabilitation of the PL route from Comilla up to the IB short of Sonamura was in progress and expected to be completed by noon of 11 Dec. He would also arrange link up with the PL route on the Indian side.

Malay had earlier briefed me about this PL route – Comilla-Sonamura and also the initiative from our side for the link up with PL Sonamura-Teliamura by our N Comn Zone Signal Regt.

Mr. Usman took us around the Exchange and introduced us to his Exchange Supervisor and AE Trunks. He also showed us the accommodation earmarked next to the Trunk Exchange for our technical staff and parking of our System Vehicle. In short, he had offered the entire comn infrastructure at Comilla; that included the local and trunk facilities along with the operating manpower.

I was impressed and was confident that with minimum effort, we could build up our rearward comn if and when our Corps HQ moved there.

Around 5-00 pm, we started our way back. It was already getting dark. We were guided to the road leading to the Indian Border towards Sonamura. The road was broad, well maintained and metalled. We must have been driving for about 20 minutes but we could not get the landmarks that we had seen while coming. It was now dark. We saw a few Pakistani soldiers fully armed walking in the same direction that we were going. At a small distance, I spotted a road barrier manned by Pak Military Police. We could also see more Pakistani soldiers. I sensed something fishy. It was obvious that we had taken the wrong direction, instead of East, we were heading West towards Mynamati Cantonment about 15 km from Comilla. I quickly reversed my jeep and turned in the direction from where we came. *That was a near miss from walking into the enemy camp.*

There were no further mishaps. We reached Sonamura RR node by 6:30 pm. I left Sub Natu and Hav Jadhav. I asked them to be prepared to move at short notice with the Systems Vehicle to Comilla; but await further instructions from me. When I reached Teliamura it was around 9:00 pm. I briefed Malay Ghosh and later my CO at our Officers' Mess. I assured him that we could provide the comn from Comilla if the Corps HQ did move there.

On 10 Dec morning, we got a call from the CSO for an urgent meeting at his office. We rushed there. The CSO mentioned about the GOC's wish that the Corps HQ should move forward and establish on the *Bangladesh soil*. He (CSO) wanted to be absolutely sure of our ability to build up the signal comn from Comilla; (The safer option was to move to our own Agartala where comn were assured but major drawback was the forward comn to Dhaka would be stretched).

My CO briefed the CSO about my visit to Comilla the previous day, the offer by the DET Comilla (Mr. Shaukat Usman), PL route build up beyond the IB from Sonamura to Comilla and our preparedness to engineer the rear comn. From my side, I confirmed the state of readiness of our System Vehicle; that it was already positioned at Sonamura ready to move to Comilla.

Brig Sidhu was pleased.

The Operation's Room was close by. Brig Sidhu asked us to accompany him there. The GOC was having a meeting with his staff, the main agenda being the Corps HQ move.

CSO went inside along with Malay and asked my CO and me to wait in the next room.

The Corps HQ offices were housed in bamboo hutments called 'bashas.' The room partitions were made of thatched bamboo panels. We could, therefore, clearly hear the proceedings in the next room where the meeting was in progress.

In his briefing, the CSO mentioned about the efforts made at Comilla on the previous three days; about Malay's visit and meeting with the

DET Comilla; the follow up visit by me; about the offer by the DET Comilla and the PL route build up to Comilla from Teliamura. He concluded,

"Sir, CO from the Corps Signal Regiment is waiting outside along with his company commander. They are also confident of providing the comn from Comilla."

GOC didn't waste any time. He said, "Gentlemen, so we move to Comilla. We close our HQ here at noon today (10 Dec) and reopen at Comilla in 48 hours later."

That was one of our proudest moments during the war; the CSO IV Corps could thus meet the operational requirements and the desire of the GOC to move the Corps HQ to Comilla (in the Bangladesh soil). All these were possible because of his (GOC) total confidence and trust in the CSO and his IV Corps Signals Team.

On 11 Dec, the advance party of the Corps HQ moved in the morning around 10:00 am for Comilla. My colleague Maj IC Singal, OC Operating Company moved with the advance elements from our Regiment.

Even before that, very early in the morning, I along with Malay left for Comilla with a few essential vehicles of the Corps HQ. Sub Natu and Hav Jadhav joined us with the Systems Vehicle en-route at Sonamura.

By 11:00 am we had reached Comilla. We deployed the Systems Vehicle next to the Trunk Exchange. To our surprise, the PL route from Sonamura to Comilla had already been patched by our Comn Zone Signals team led by Maj J M Khullar and by the DET staff at Comilla. What more, they had already tested the Comilla - Sonamura - PL route up to Teliamura. The Carrier and VFT equipment of the P& T type all brand new in our System Vehicle behaved superbly. It is to the credit of IV Corps Signals that even before arrival of the Advance Party, the systems were put through from Comilla to our Teliamura Carrier Center and a few trunk speech channels were extended beyond to Shillong, Calcutta and Delhi.

The real test however, was deriving the speech and telegraph channels and meticulously patching these to get direct circuits from

Comilla to Shillong, Calcutta, Delhi and other cities in the Corps Comn Zone as per the scale. Since Malay Ghosh was there at Comilla end, to take care of the comn, I decided to return to Teliamura to oversee the work at the Carrier station at Teliamura. By 03:00 pm I was back.

Thus, we had ensured active presence of our best personnel at both ends of this vital link. At the Comilla end, we had two of our most competent technical stalwarts in Sub Natu and Hav Jadhav under my colleague Maj Ghosh (SO2 Signals); At the Teliamura end, we had Sub Maj Kalidas, F of S, in Charge Carrier Center and his highly motivated team (2). They all knew the equipment, which they had been handling in the Carrier Center ever since the beginning. I was there at the Teliamura Carrier Centre the whole evening till late night and witnessed the dedication and the technical competence of our Signals mechanics; indeed, all of them without exception made us proud.

By midnight, a large majority of the speech and telegraph channels were patched, tested and handed over to the respective trunk exchanges or the Signal Centre.

DET Comilla kept his promise. He had his essential staff and the operators on duty when the Advance party of the Corps HQ arrived late in the night. By then important trunk circuits had already been extended to the Trunk Exchange.

Maj I C Singal, on arrival at Comilla quickly took control of both the local and trunk exchanges. He arranged to extend a few essential connections from the Local Auto Exchange to the senior Corps Staff. The Corps Comdr came to Comilla in the evening sometimes and in the night, he made a few calls including one to his home at Jaipur.

By morning on 12 Dec, the Corps comn at Comilla had been fully established. Bulk of the Corps HQ and our Regiment arrived on 12 Dec. By noon 12 Dec 1971 HQ IV Corps reopened from Comilla well ahead of the schedule.

POST SCRIPT

I had recommended Sub Maj Kalidas, Naib Sub Dinkar Natu and Hav Jadhav for gallantry awards immediately after the War. If my memory serves me right, they were the only few from our Regiment to get some awards; I do not recall, may be 'Mentioned in Dispatches' or 'Chief of Army Staff Commendation.'

Malay Ghosh's Side of the Story *(continued from p 51)*

Move of Corps HQ to Comilla (night 9 Dec to 11 Dec 1971)

That night (9 Dec) I was rung up by the CSO at around 1030 pm. He told me that the GOC had desired during dinner at the A mess that the Corps HQ must be established on Bangladesh soil by the evening of 11 Dec. I suggested that the COs of IV Corps Sig Regt and N Comn Z Sig Regt be called immediately for a meeting. I went to the CSO immediately and told him that we could move to Comilla where the Corps HQ could be located at the Circuit House premises. The Civil Exchange can then be taken over and comn extended from there. The system vehicles containing both the Army and P&T type carrier systems were ready at Sonamura and could be moved forward so that rearward comn could be extended by mounting the same on PL pairs that now existed up to Comilla after patching up of routes at Belonia. I also said that the Task should be entrusted to Maj Narayanan and that Signal elements should move accordingly before dawn (11 Dec). I would accompany Maj Narayanan so that matters could be sorted out with the DET and his cooperation ensured. The matter was discussed with the COs who had arrived by then and the move plan was agreed to.

We accordingly started in the early hours of the morning (11 Dec) at 0400 am with a small convoy of signals and a few advance elements from the Corps HQ. We reached Comilla around 0800h in the morning (10 Dec). By noon, essential rear trunk speech comns had been provided to Teliamura carrier centre. In the meantime, Tele Instruments of Siemens type (obtained from the DET) had been connected in all the rooms at the Circuit House along with a directory and instructions for users with each Phone. The Corps HQ elements arrived in the afternoon and started functioning by the evening.

The GOC arrived in the evening (11 Dec) and asked to be put through to his family at Jaipur. The Call was connected immediately and we felt happy that Signals have very successfully risen to the occasion.

PART III

Signal Comn Efforts by IV Corps Signals at Dhaka: 17 and 18 Dec 1971

The safety and honour of your country come first, always and every time.
The safety and honour of the men you command come next, always and every time
Your own safety and well-being come last, always and every time."

—Engraving in Chetwood Hall,
Indian Military Academy, Dehradun

9

Airlift from Comilla to Dhaka: 16 Dec 1971

On 12 Dec 1971 at noon, HQ IV Corps reopened at Comilla well ahead of the Corps Commander's deadline.

On 16 Dec evening, the Pakistan Eastern Army Command surrendered. Some essential elements of HQ IV Corps moved to Dhaka on the evening of 17 Dec 1971. Bulk of the Corps HQ however remained at Comilla till 20th Dec when it moved to Mynamathi, the Cantonment town of Comilla.

During this period at Comilla, the signal comn had never been so good. Comilla Exchange enabled us to provide telephones with auto dialing facility and that was a welcome change to the Corps staff after having been used to the operator assisted manual exchange at Teliamura. Our 'Systems Vehicle' virtually extended the trunk circuits from Teliamura. We had also shifted the RR node from *Sonamura to Comilla* and established a single hop RR link to Teliamura as 'standby' to line (PL). There was a spate of private calls to the families left behind in the peace stations. Many of these calls were routed via the Army HQ Delhi trunks.

> *One significant achievement was providing an RR link to 'Advance HQ' established by 23 Div for control of the operations by 83 Bde and K Force on the Feni-Chitagong axis to secure Chittagong. This was on 13/14 Dec. We could provide this vital RR comn through Comilla RR node in conjunction with Aijal node. Our RR to the formation HQ during this phase never failed. Capt Tamhane was in charge of the RR dets. (See Appendix 4-Reminiscences of Bangladesh War 1971 by Col T D Tamhane (retd.)*

On 16 Dec 1971 at Comilla, from early morning, the atmosphere was charged with the rumour about surrender of the Pakistan Army. Unfortunately, HQ Eastern Command had not planned the comn from Dhaka to Calcutta or Delhi, a lapse more due to the rapid nature of the operations and the fall of Dhaka much earlier than anticipated.

We were eagerly waiting for news from Dhaka, which was trickling down, in bits and pieces. There was a lot of excitement, tension and anxiety. Around 8 am my CSO called me.

"Naru, I am flying with the GOC to Dhaka. We have to be in the helipad in the next one hour.

"Sir, any formal news about the surrender?"

CSO: I really don't know, nor does the GOC. I want a mobile radio set with a radio operator to go with me. Have an operator at your end and be on 24-hour listening watch. I will call you on the Radio link from Dhaka when I come to know."

We had anticipated this requirement and had earmarked appropriate radio set (Man-pack HF Radio Set GR 345). We had even improvised an antenna mount for use inside the GOC's helicopter for comn during the flight.

There was practically no contact with Brig Sidhu for the next 24 hours. We heard about the surrender and the formal surrender ceremony late in the night through AIR broadcast.

Around 11.00 am on 17 Dec, my radio operator called me. CSO was on the air. Being a simplex radio, we had to follow the procedure of 'Over' after every transmission and go on the 'receive' mode.

This was what my CSO said:

> *"Here everything is topsy-turvy. There is no trunk circuit from the exchange here to Calcutta or Delhi or for that matter to any Indian city. I want you here immediately with a small comn detachment. One helicopter is coming there by 3 pm and it will pick you up on its return. We have to establish our own IV Corps RR from Dhaka to Comilla for access to Shillong via Teliamura. (1). See what you can do about this before you leave."*

I informed my CO and had an emergency meeting with *Capt Nirmal Dhillon* - OC RR, *Lt Tarun Mahendra* - *OC Radio and Sub Natu* - *OC Systems.*

I also had *Capt Tushar Tamhane,* that bright young officer attached from Bravo Corps Signal Regt (a newly raised signal unit), in the meeting. He had just returned after his RR det had put through that vital RR speech circuit for Chitagong operation. The following was decided:

- *Capt Tamhane* to establish a RR repeater at Daudkandi (on the East Bank of *R Meghna*); the terminal for the forward link to Dhaka kept on 24 hour listening watch to respond to RR signals from Dhaka terminal as and when it opens; (see sketch map)
- OC systems to engineer dedicated circuits to Calcutta and Delhi when RR to Dhaka gets through

I was aware that our two formation RR terminals were on the move and would reach Dhaka sometimes in the evening. I planned to use one of these that arrived first. I collected the matching frequency crystals for use at the Dhaka end.

As regards the detachment to go with me to Dhaka, I had my pick of mechanics (telegraph, radio and line), radio operators, and of course my trusted driver Sigmn Barkat Ram. Hav Jadhav my systems expert was the NCO in charge, in all nine of them.

We were at the Helipad by 2.30 pm. The helicopter landed sharp at 3.00 pm. and we were airborne within 15 minutes. Our flight took us across the mighty Meghna River; the view from the air was awesome. We could see a very long line of vehicles waiting at the pontoon bridge/ ferry site near Daudkandi; an uncomfortable thought crossed my mind that our formation RR terminal vehicles might also be stuck there in that long queue waiting for their turn.

As our helicopter was approaching *Dhaka,* we could see long convoys of military vehicles on the trunk roads converging towards the Capital city. Over the *Dhaka-Tejgaon Military Airport,* we saw a few craters on the main runway caused by our Air Force strikes, a few aircraft stranded on ground; also, thousands of men and women with flags waving at us. We landed at one corner of the Airfield, a km away from the Airport terminal.

It was only after we landed and the pilot had switched off the engine, that we could hear the shout of the people, 'Joi Bangla' repeatedly, the

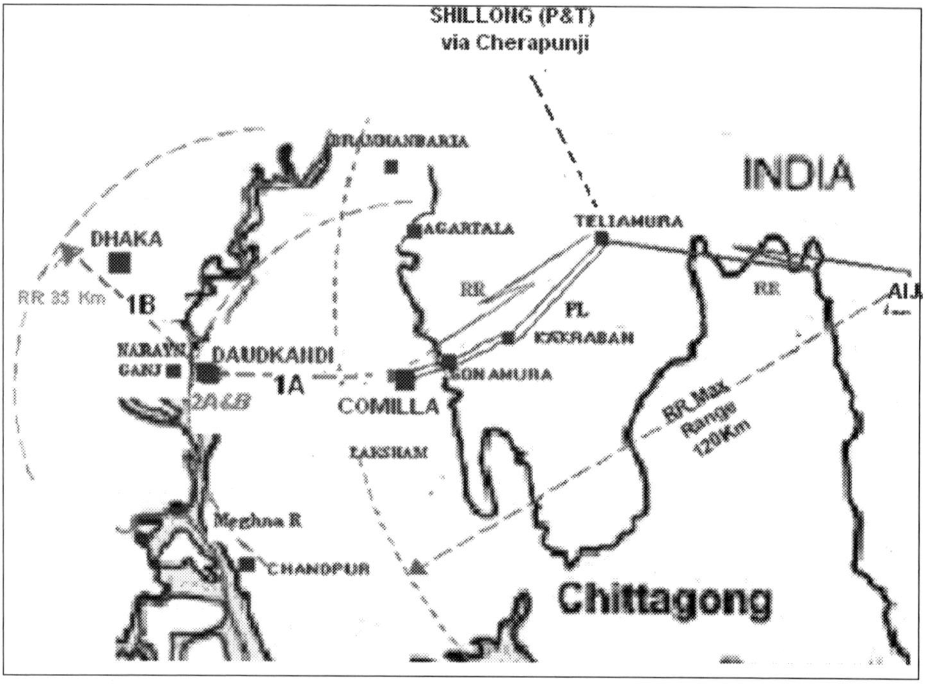

Planning for the RR build up from Comilla to Dhaka: 1500 hrs 17 Dec 1971

1. *RR Dets under Capt Tamhane to move to Daudkandi and establish RR repeater by 1800 hrs.17 Dec1971. From Daudkandi:*
   - 1A—Rear RR link to Comilla;
   - 1B—Forward RR link to Dhaka.
2. *Capt Tamhane* to keep vigil and await Dhaka RR terminal to come up on air (by midnight). Two RR Terminals **2A & B** under *Nb Sub Saini (Naik Vittal the det. in charge)* waiting at the ferry crossing to move to DHAKA soonest and report to Maj Narayanan at E Pak Military HQ at Dhaka.

sound laden with excitement piercing the air; it must have been around 4.30 pm exactly 24 hours after signing of the instrument of surrender.

Here is my recall of the few moments at the Dhaka Airport on that historic evening of 17 Dec 1971.

> *4.00 – 4.30 pm*
>
> *We walk down to the Terminal Building hauling our baggage. We are surrounded by a big crowd; men, women and children; all in a festive mode. They look at us with curiosity, and respect, as their saviors and liberators. They all shout, Joi Bangla again and again.*

4.45- 5.00 pm
I look for some transport to take us to the Cantonment area. A closed van arrives. Six or seven ladies wearing burka (veil covering the face) and a couple of men get down. They all are excited to see us, the Indian soldiers. I politely ask the elderly gentleman, "Sir, where is the Army cantonment area? We need to go there."
He replies, "Janab" (Sir), It's about 7 to 8 miles. You take our van and get yourself dropped at the Cantonment. We can wait. It's an honor to be of some assistance to you." He gives instructions to his driver. I was touched by their friendly attitude and eagerness to help. It was our proud moment, being treated with respect and honor by the citizens of the just born Nation, 'Bangladesh.'

It was around 5 pm, when we got into the van; I took the co-driver's seat. The Road from the Airport to the Cantonment area was broad and in good shape, but it was jam packed with our own Army vehicles of the Indian Army units and formations who had raced to Dhaka and now homing on to the cantonment area in search of accommodation.

On either side of the Road, Pakistani soldiers were walking in single file, all in uniform and carrying their weapons, with their heads down and not knowing their fate. More than elation of a *victor*, I was overwhelmed with sympathy for these soldiers of the Pakistan Army vanquished in War; all marching to the Prisoners of War (POW) camps set up in the cantonment.

It took us 45 minutes to reach the Pakistan Eastern Command HQ. The campus looked very imposing and modern. We found our way to the Signal Center and Exchange building. It was spacious and was well laid out. We looked for the rest rooms meant for the shift personnel; found a few next to the Military Exchange; took two of them and dumped our luggage. I released the van after thanking the Driver. Later I came to know that the Receiver Station was also located in the same building

The time was 6.30 pm on 17 Dec 1971; here I was, at the erstwhile Pakistan Eastern Command HQ Signal Center at Dhaka, just a day after the 'birth of the new Nation' – "Bangladesh".

As I was looking around the Signal Center, I saw Brig Sidhu, my CSO in an adjoining building. He called me and said, *"Good, that you are here. CSO Command is having a meeting. Come with me"*.

10

Signal Comn from Dhaka: Challenges

During war (or hostile environment), anticipate several steps ahead; yet plan for the worst lest you are taken by surprise.

It was a conference room. Brig K K Tiwari, the CSO Eastern Command was seated. There were a number of signal officers; some from the staff and mostly from the signal units of formations that had raced to Dhaka from all sectors; of course, they all were OC units (lieutenant colonels or senior majors). It's over 35 years and I recall only a few names: Maj AJS Gill and Major B K Kataria both staff officers to Brig Tiwari, my own CSO Brig Sidhu and Malay Ghosh. I don't remember any others who were present. I was aware that till then (evening of 17 Dec 1971), Army signal comn from Dhaka to Calcutta and Delhi had not been established. Brig Tiwari was looking tense.

When he saw me with Brig Sidhu, he perhaps assumed that essential elements of IV Corps Signal Regiment had already arrived at Dhaka. He gave me the following tasks:

1. *Take control of the Transmitter Station of the Pakistan Eastern Army Command and establish the following radio links to Delhi and Calcutta with assistance from Pak Signals personnel:*
   - *A7 Radio Telegraphy link to Army HQ Delhi.*
   - *E5 Radio Telegraphy link to HQ Eastern Command Calcutta.*
2. *Establish RR link Dhaka – Comilla – Teliamura and integrate with the Department of Telecommunication (DOT) network for comn to Delhi and Calcutta.*

   (See sketch map next page for easy comprehension of the tasks on hand)

CSO Command wanted me to complete the above tasks before sunrise the next morning. He was in no mood to listen to my CSO or me. He wanted me to get on with the job immediately. I came out of the Meeting. (Rather pushed out of the Meeting!). For a moment I didn't know what was happening? I was wondering, "With a small signal detachment and in an unfamiliar place like Dhaka, how am I going to complete the tasks given to me with no resources? And I am supposed to take assistance from Pakistani PW – Signals personnel. I don't even have a vehicle."

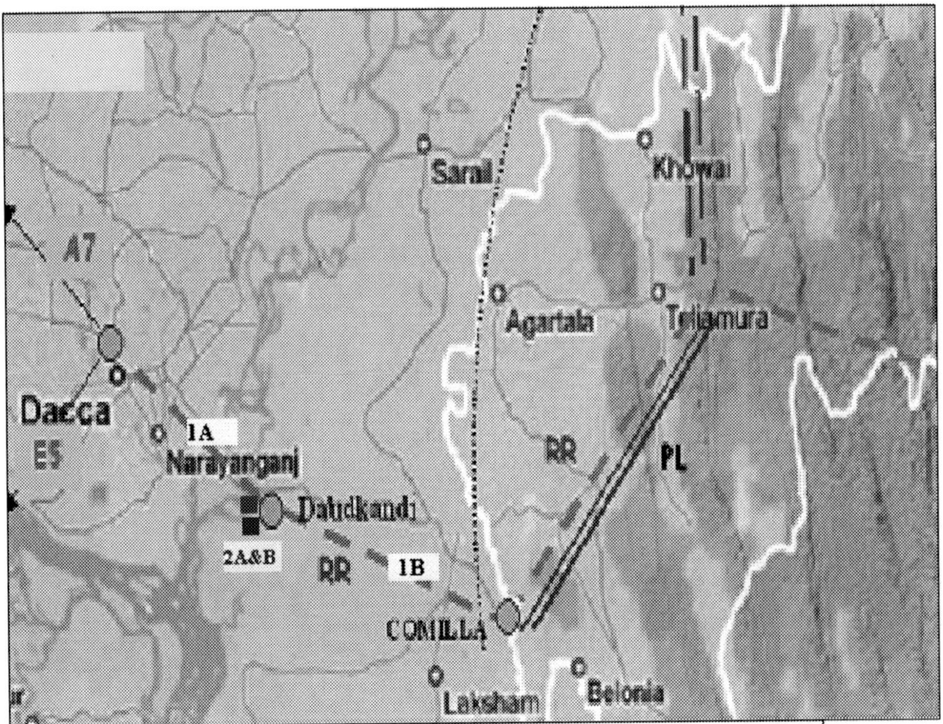

←30 km→

Courtesy: Google Map

Tasks given by CSO Command at Dhaka: 1830 hrs 17 Dec (to complete by 0600 hrs 18 Dec '71)

- ***A7 Radio Telegraphy*** *link to Army HQ Delhi*
- ***E5 Radio Telegraphy*** *link to HQ Eastern Command Calcutta.*
- *Establish* ***RR link: Dhaka–Comilla–Teliamura*** *and integrate with the* DOT network for comn to Delhi and Calcutta

Legend: 1A and 1B: RR link Dhaka–Daudkandi–Comilla
2A & B Our RR terminals at the Ferry site

One consolation however was that we had anticipated and planned the rearwards RR comn from Dhaka (1A & 1B) but my anxiety was, how soon our two RR terminals at the Daudkani ferry site (2A&B) would get their turn to cross and reach Dhaka.'

While I was thus musing over the tasks in hand, Brig Sidhu came out. He tried to put me at ease, "Naru, I can understand your difficulties. CSO Command is under tremendous pressure. We have to do whatever possible to support him. There is no point in raising any issues with him now. Go to the Transmitter Station and I am sure you will find someone from the Pakistani Signals to assist you."

I just moaned, "Sir, I don't even have a vehicle?" His answer was, "Take anyone from these abandoned vehicles by the Pakistan Army. I am myself using one of them. Petrol should be no problem. You will find every vehicle having spare jerry cans with petrol."

As he turned back to return to the meeting, he said in a consoling tone, "Naru, don't worry, do whatever is possible. I have full confidence in you".

11

Signal Comn Efforts at Dhaka: 6.00 pm 17 Dec to Midnight 17/18 Dec 1971

Develop the attitude to look at every adverse situation as an opportunity and take full advantage.

It was 6.00 pm. I asked *Hav Jadhav* to assemble all our men and get someone senior from the Pakistani Signal Corps. Within 5 minutes, one Pakistani NCO came with *Jadhav*. My men in the meantime had assembled. I briefed them on the tasks given and what I expected from each one of them. The Pak NCO was also present during the briefing. (I don't remember his name). I asked him about the Transmitter Station. He replied, "Janab, It is 5 miles down the main road. If you like, I can send one of my men to guide you." When I probed further, he said, "Sir, I am from the Receiver Station here in this building (Signal Centre). We are 8 of us here. Our NCO in charge is *Hav Guldast*; he went to the PW Camp at 5.00 pm and we are waiting for his return. After that we may also be required to go to the PW camp." From his body language, I could sense that he was worried about their safety and eager to go to the PW camp soonest. I told him politely but firmly, "Naik, I want you and your men here to help us establish the radio links. As soon as *Hav Guldast* returns, he should report to me. I assure you that you all will be treated like my own men. You will be relieved as soon as we complete our tasks. I also assure your safety."

I had the choice to pick up any vehicle from the abandoned fleet consisting of jeeps, land rovers, assortment of cars mostly Volkswagen. I, however, preferred a jeep; my driver Barkat Ram picked up a fairly new jeep with the assistance from the Pak Naik. He also collected a couple of jerry cans of petrol. It was 7.00 pm. We were on our way to the Transmitter Station with one of the Pak soldiers as our guide.

7.30 pm to 10.00 pm

The road was deserted. It was pitch dark. There wasn't any traffic. I liked the sound of the engine from my smooth-running jeep. But soon we started hearing stray Sten gun shots.

I didn't pay much attention as I was totally focused on the tasks in hand. We reached in about 30 minutes. The transmitter building was impressive and looked much similar to our own static transmitter stations at the command and corps level. When I entered the portico, I was in for a great surprise; a Pakistani Signals JCO along with one of our own JCO was there to receive me.

Sub Riaz gave a smart salute and introduced himself as OC Transmitters. The other JCO was Sub Amaranth Mehta* (*that's how I remember his name). Sub Mehta had accompanied Maj AJS Gill, SO2 Signals Eastern Command earlier in the evening. He (Gill) had given two sets of High Frequency (HF) one for A7 to Delhi and the other for E5 to Calcutta, and told that someone responsible would be joining them to give further instructions. Well that 'someone' happened to be me!

There were over a dozen medium and high-power transmitters mostly *British SWAB8 (Marconi)* and *Siemens 1 KW.* These were well laid out. There were two other Pak soldiers obviously radio mechanics. Sub Riaz preferred *Siemens 1 KW to the old vintage SWAB8*. I was well conversant with the Siemens Transmitter. I felt encouraged. Our immediate task was to design the sky wave aerials for the given frequencies and get them erected with compatible masts, an arduous task in that late hour of the night. Here is a brief account of our efforts in regard to the two links:

A7 Delhi Radio Telegraph (RTg) Link

Sub Riaz mentioned that they were using Siemens 1 KW for their *Rawalpindi link* using rhombic aerial. Rhombic aerial[1] is a broadband antenna with directional gain. It occurred to me, "why not use this for

Signal Comn at Dhaka (ni 17/18 Dec 1971): Tasks and Efforts
Commence: 4:00 pm 17 Dec Tasks Completed upto 1130 pm

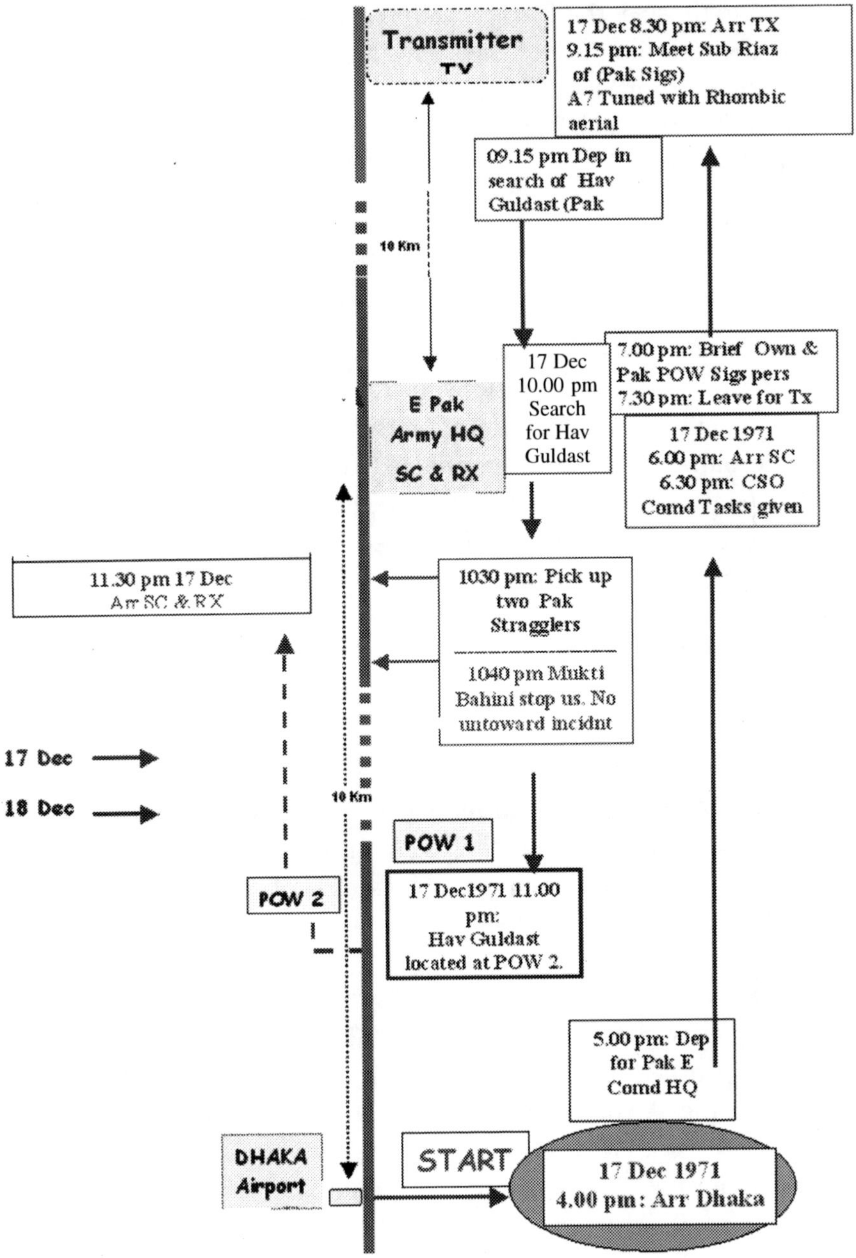

Delhi A7 link since *Dhaka–Rawalpindi* and *Dhaka–Delhi* directions were close." I checked the frequencies and fortunately A7 frequencies were also close to those of the *Rawalpindi link*. We decided to try and tune the *Siemens 1 KW* transmitter to the A7 night frequency. The two Pak radio mechanics in a matter of few minutes tuned the Transmitter with the same rhombic antenna. Thus, this innovation was successful in saving us time and effort.

We now had the real problem. There was no way of knowing whether our RF signals were being received by Army HQ Receivers at Delhi since we had no comn with the Dhaka Receiver Station.

Normally there are a number of dedicated cable pairs between Transmitter and Receiver stations for remote controlling the Trans and Receive functions by the operator on the link. *Sub Riaz* mentioned that the cable pairs had been disconnected from the Signal Center end a couple of days back and that only *Hav Guldast*, OC Receivers would be able to restore these and the dedicated one to one telephone to the Receiver Station.

E5 Calcutta–RTg Link

We couldn't use an existing aerial since none was directed towards South or South West for us to take a chance for Calcutta link. We decided to erect a dipole aerial in the space available next to the car park. Masts were available at the Transmitter Station but all other stores including the aerial wire were at the Receivers, and we had to get these from there. Our priority, therefore, was to locate Hav Guldast, NCO in charge Receivers.

10.00 pm to 11.59 pm (midnight 17 Dec 1971)

We had to first check at the Signal centre if *Hav Guldast* had come; otherwise proceed to the PW camp to locate him. I asked Sub Riaz to accompany me. We first stopped at the Signal Centre. *Hav Guldast* hadn't returned till then. We drove on the wide road in the pitched darkness. I was wondering, "What strange happenings in the last 12 hours; here I am, an Indian Army officer with a Pakistani JCO driving on the roads of Dhaka: both from respective Corps of Signals of the two warring countries, brought together to put through important radio links for the Indian Army."

We heard short bursts of Sten gun shots away from the road; I had earlier heard that Pak soldiers were permitted to carry their arms to defend themselves from the *Mukti Bahini* soldiers who were gunning for them. We saw two Pak soldiers (stragglers) walking slowly on the road, tired and exhausted, towards the PW camps. Sub Riaz with hesitation asked, *"Sir, can we drop them at the POW Camp? They may get killed if they are seen by Mukti Bahini troops."*

I stopped the jeep and asked the soldiers to get in. First, they were scared, but on seeing Sub Riaz, felt safe. We drove for another few minutes. Sure enough, we were stopped by a group of *Mukti Bahini* soldiers. I put a comforting hand on Sub Riaz's shivering arm. One of them, a Lieutenant showed his torchlight first on *Sub Riaz*. Recognising him (as a Pak soldier) his first reaction was to get furious but when he turned the torchlight on me, he immediately recognised me from my uniform and badges of rank, gave me a smart salute. He asked me politely, "Sir, who are these Pak soldiers"? I replied, "*Bandhu (I had learnt this Bengali word at Comilla to mean a close relative)* they are from the Eastern Command Transmitter Station. We have to put through important radio links to Calcutta and Delhi most urgently. We need their help". He didn't say anything but gave me a smart salute and I drove forward.

In a few minutes, we reached one of the PW camps. We stopped at the gate; Pak soldiers were manning it. One of them came running and saluted smartly. When queried about *Hav Guldast*, he replied, *"Janab, this camp is for the JCOs. The OR Camp is further a mile down the road."* In another 10 minutes, we reached the second PW Camp. We left the two Pak Soldiers there.

The sentry at the gate went in to enquire about *Hav Guldast*. In less than 5 minutes, *Hav Guldast* appeared. He looked tired and scared. When he saw *Sub Riaz*, he felt comfortable. When I briefed him about our mission, his response was spontaneous:

> *"Sir, I will be with you in 5 minutes. We have not had anything to eat since yesterday. Some food has been cooked and being served now. Can I collect some?"*

Signal Comn at Dhaka (ni 17/18 Dec 1971): Tasks and Efforts
Commence: 4:00 pm 17 Dec Close: 6:30 am 18 Dec

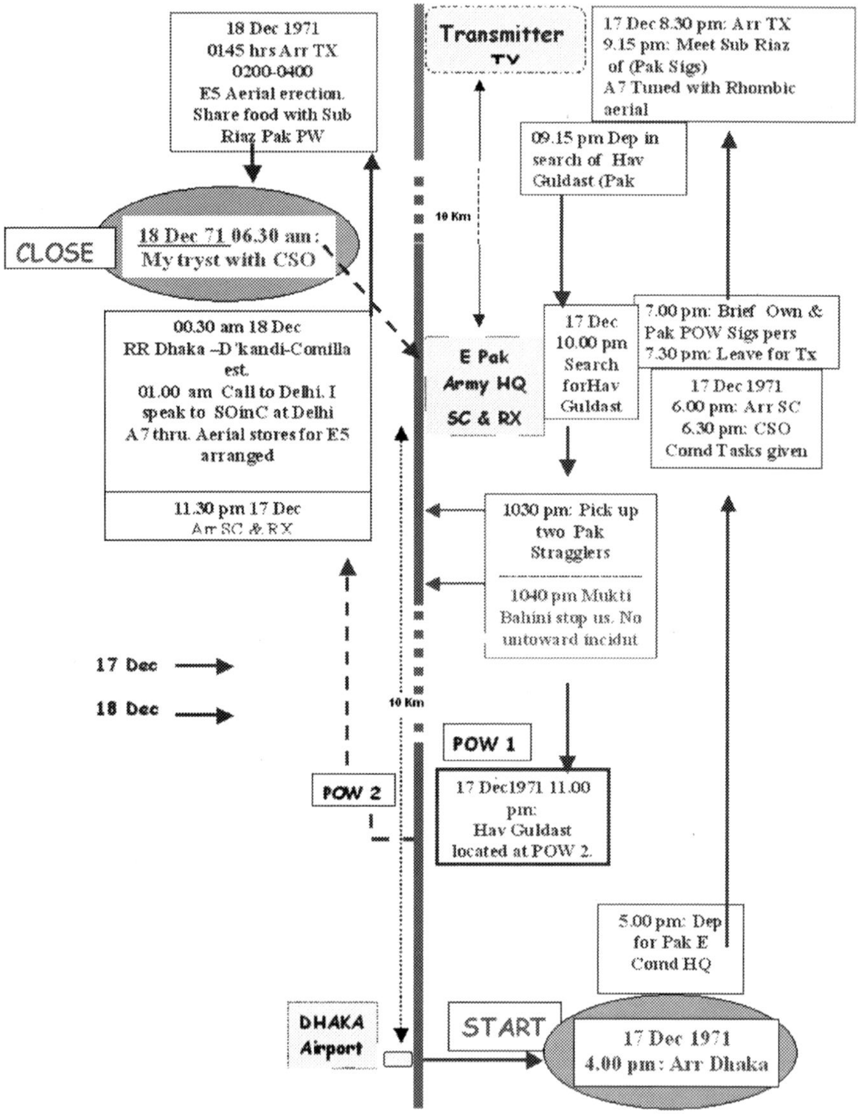

He returned in 5 minutes with two small aluminum vessels filled with rice and dhal.

> *"Janab, these are for my colleagues in the Receiver Station who are waiting for me."*

We headed back. As we were about to cross the first PW camp, *Sub Riaz* with some hesitation made a similar request, *"Sir, May I also collect some food for my men in the transmitter station."* I nodded. He returned in a few minutes with a couple of mess tins and a small vessel filled with rice and dhal. When we reached the Signal Center (Receiver Station), it was 11.30 pm.

Hav Guldast didn't waste a moment. He restored a few cable pairs and the direct one to one telephone to the Transmitter. *Sub Riaz* in the meantime identified and segregated the aerial stores required at the Transmitter Station for the E5 dipole aerial. I sent my radio operators to man the receivers for A7 and E5. I was happy with the progress made and what more I knew that in those few hours, I had won the confidence and the trust of the soldiers of the Pakistan Signal Corps. I also realised that I had to live up to their trust and ensure their safety.

I asked my Driver *Barkat Ram* to drop Sub Riaz with the aerial stores at the transmitter station and return.

It was midnight 17/18 Dec 1971.

NOTE

1. **Rhombic antenna** is one of the most popular fixed-station antennas, useful in point-to-point comn over a wide frequency range. It is a broadband directional antenna, mostly used in HF, also called short wave. It is WIDELY used for long-distance transmission and reception.

12

RR Comn from Dhaka to Comilla: Midnight 17/18 Dec 1971

It was midnight 17/18 Dec 1971 when I left the Receiver hall.

When I came to the Signal Center, I saw a few press and media persons including one Russian correspondent waiting. They all had messages to be sent to Delhi or Calcutta. I promised them that the Delhi RTg link was getting established and that we would certainly accept important messages for clearance.

As I came out of the Signal Center, even in that darkness, I could see a lonely figure approaching me. As he came near, I recognised him. He was Naik Vittal, RR Det Comdr of one of our formation. He managed to get his RR vehicle across the Meghna River at Daudkandi around 9.00 pm. He had come straight to Dhaka and found his way to the Signal center. He said, *"Sir, Nb Sub Nasib Singh is with the other RR terminal and they were still in the waiting line at the ferry crossing."* I felt greatly relieved. Naik Vittal, and his two other Det personnel, were looking extremely tired. I asked them to park the RR vehicle in the car park next to the Exchange.

Hav Jadhav got them some tea and snacks. I gave *Naik Vittal* the frequency crystals that I was safely carrying; asked him to put up the antenna masts with the boom directed towards Daudkandi. In a matter of about 30 minutes, the two antenna masts (transmit and the Receive) were up. The Transmitter was first tuned and as the receiver was in the process, we could see the 'RF monitor pointer' moving towards full scale. I could hear through audio speaker the voice of *Capt Tamhane.*

"Sir, can you hear me? I have been waiting for your call since 6.00 pm (1); I am through to Comilla and Teliamura Trunks from here."

He also mentioned that he had sited the RR relay station on a mound overlooking the River; that it was a km away from the ferry/pontoon bridge site and that there were a large number of Pak soldiers walking back towards *Mynamati-Comilla* and all of them were fully armed. I complimented *Tushar* and his team for their dedication and commitment. I also asked him keep away from the Pak soldiers and not worry about them as their only aim could be to retreat to the safety of their *Mynamati* Garrison. I however cautioned him not to venture out till morning by which time the area would be clear. (*Please see* ***Note 1*** *for Capt Tushar Tamhane's side of the story)*.

In the meantime, *Naik Vittal* connected the multi-channel carrier equipment and extended the channels to the Military Trunk Exchange (Dhaka). My immediate worry was the Delhi A7 link. I asked for OC Army HQ Transmitters Delhi. That was connected in no time. (See sketch Map.)

Maj Natarajan one of my close colleagues came up on the line. He was excited to get a call from Dhaka. "Naru, we are already on listening watch on A7. I shall attend to it. SO-in-C is anxious to know about signal comn from Dhaka. He would be happy to speak to you."

Just then Hav Jadhav rushed to say that A7 was through. This I communicated to Maj Natarajan. He then got the call transferred to the SO-in-C. The ring was passing. I was nervously waiting for Lt Gen E G Pettengel, SO-in-C.

SO-in-C came up on the line:

> *"Who's that? What's happening?*
> *"Sir, I am Maj Narayanan of IV Corps Signals speaking from Dhaka.. Sorry to disturb you at this odd hour. We established this RR link from Dhaka a few minutes back. This call to Delhi has been put through our Corps carrier at Comilla. We are also through on the A7 RTg link to Army HQ."*
> *SO in C: Where is the CSO Command?"*
> *"Sir, I met him in the evening at 6.00 pm. I frankly do not know where he is or how to contact him. The Military Exchange here is not functional."*

SO in C: "Ask CSO Comd to call me first thing in the morning."

The time was 1.00 am 18 Dec 1971.

I strongly believe that these were the first few calls from Dhaka to Delhi via an Army channel provided by IV Corps Signals on the night 17/18 Dec 1971, a fact not recorded or recognised in any document or history related to the Bangladesh War 1971.

Thus, I had completed two out of the three tasks given to me by the CSO Command. Establishing Radio link A7 to Delhi and RR link to Comilla for integrating the Army trunk circuit to the National grid via Shillong.

I had yet one more task, 'to put through E5-RTg link to Calcutta.'

Capt Tushar Tamhane's Side of the Story

RR Comn to Dhaka – Relay at Daudkandi- 17 Dec 1971

On 17 Dec in the morning at Comilla, Maj Narayanan tasked me to establish a RR relay at Duadkhandi on the east bank of the Meghna River by 1800 hours (17 Dec) and be on the listening watch awaiting RR signal from him from Dhaka. At the Daudkandi ferry site, a pontoon bridge had been earlier established to cross the river en-route to Dhaka. I moved the RR dets to Daudkhandi during the morning and reached our destination well before sun set; since the bridge site was on the river bank, it was not suitable for obtaining the required RLOS (FFZ clearance). I didn't want to take a chance of setting up a marginal RR link; I scouted the area and located a mound. It was about a Km away from the bridge site. Although it lacked inherent defence and fire support from our troops at the pontoon bridge site, it was ideally suited for RR communications. The RR link to Comilla was established without any problem. The RR terminal for the link to Dhaka was tuned and kept ready and on listening watch as per instructions. Having completed our primary task, I set about to coordinate our defences as we were away from bridgehead. After earmarking the defensive perimeter fire trenches, I proceeded to the bridge site and informed the OC Troops there of our location and the purpose of our being there; we then arranged mutual fire support between our two locations. During this period, I saw a movement of Pak troops fully armed in large numbers and I cautioned my men to be on guard and alert.

I had thus completed my task well in time and we patiently waited for the

RR det Dhaka to come on air. Around midnight (17 Dec), the RF monitor showed a flicker, all personnel in the det were alert and anxious. As soon as the radio was tuned, ***Maj Narayanan*** *came up on the air. It was a pleasure listening to him. I did query him on the delay. He explained the situation at his (Dhaka) end; he congratulated the efforts of our relay dets. After the radio patch was extended from Dhaka to Comilla, we breathed a sigh of relief, having successfully accomplished our mission.*

See Appendix 4: Reminiscences Bangladesh War 1971 by Col (retd.) T D Tamahane.

13

Signal Comn from Dhaka: Midnight 17/18 Dec to 0630 am 18 Dec 1971

"Honour, safety and the dignity of prisoners of war placed under you should also be of equal concern always and every time."

—Suggested addition to the engravings in Chetwood Hall, IMA Dehradun

I had yet one more task, 'to put through E5-RTg link to Calcutta.'

With the RR and A7 under control, I asked Hav Jadhav to supervise these; Hav Guldast in the meantime had collected some more stores indicated by Sub Riaz. I thought he would be useful at the Transmitters for aerial erection and asked him to come with me. We were back at the Transmitter Station by 2.00 am. By then Sub Riaz had done all the preliminary design work for the E5 link. He left the actual installation to Hav Guldast. He gave a surprise. "Sir, I have selected the place for erection in the area adjoining the car park. It is safe here. Last week, our Engineers had laid some mines inside the aerial park."

After seeing the site and progress on the aerial erection, we returned to the Transmitter hall. Sub Riaz gave me yet another surprise. He had not taken his food, till then. His two-radio mechanics however had taken their food. He obviously was waiting for me. "Sir, you yourself look very tired. Perhaps you also have NOT eaten anything since morning. Would you care to share some food with us, whatever we have?" Although my first reaction was to give some excuse, I saw in his eyes *'the God deep within'* and I couldn't refuse.

I vividly recall those few precious minutes at the Transmitter Station at Dhaka around 2.00 am on 18 Dec 1971. As a token of respect to Sub Riaz's sentiments, I took a spoon of rice and dhal that he offered from the mess tin that he had earlier collected before leaving the Pak PW camp. There was no animosity, no ill will; I couldn't see any difference at that time between an Indian and a Pakistani soldier; our few hours' association in trying circumstances had created a deep bond transgressing suspicions and hatred due to religious or political differences.

As we were engaged in a conversation, Sub Riaz with a worried look said, "Sir, I have five daughters. My wife always remains sick. In the last two years, I have not gone on leave. What will happen to us-the prisoners of war?" I assured him that every one of them would be safe with the Indian Army; they would be treated with honour and dignity, repatriated back to Pakistan once the political settlement process was completed.

Hav Guldast joined us to give us the progress on E5 aerial, that it would take another 30 to 45 minutes to complete the installation. I asked him an innocuous question, "Guldast, how is that you have not damaged your equipment to prevent their falling into our (your enemy's) hands?"

He gave a touching reply, "Sir, I have been with these transmitters for the past 1½ years. I have not seen anything else during this period. How can I destroy these equipments, which are as dear to me as my own children?" (1)

Sub Riaz added, "Sir, You can appreciate the work load on the Corps of Signals units. I have been OC Transmitters for the last one-year and have been working here day and night along with my men. We have not seen anything else during this period nor do we know what has been happening outside."

He also made some profound remarks:

> *"Sir, I am proud to belong to the Pakistan Army Signal Corps. Our signalmen or for that matter our soldiers are as good as yours. But the major difference is the gap between our officers and OR; I couldn't believe that Indian Army officers like you are so easily approachable and the*

consideration you show to your men and even to us" (implying your enemy)

These words from a Pakistani JCO made me proud to be an officer of the Indian Army.

I couldn't help recalling the famous engraving in Chetwood Hall at the Indian Military Academy, Dehra Dun, from where I passed out as a commissioned officer in 1957.

It reads:

"The safety and honor of your country come first, always and every time.
The safety and honor of the men you command come next, always and every time
Your own safety and well-being comes last, always and every time."

I am proud that in those hours of glory, having defeated the East Pakistani Army comprehensively, Indian Army went out of the way to protect the lives of Pak soldiers and treated them with honour and dignity. I strongly feel that we should consider adding to the Chetwood engraving thus:

"Honour, safety and the dignity of prisoners of war placed under you should also be of equal concern always and every time."

The time was 4.00 am. Hav Guldast had completed the aerial installation. We had to run the antenna feeder cables inside the building through the ducts exiting into the Aerial Park. Sub Riaz said, "Sir, the cable feeder area is safe from mines. Please come with me. I will go in front of you." By 5.00 am, the E 5 transmitter (also a Siemens 1 KW) had been tuned.

Now, I had to get back with Hav Guldast to the Receivers.

Time was 0530 a.m. We were in the Receiver hall. Hav Guldast got busy to establish the E 5 link to Calcutta.

The Delhi-A7 was already through and the link was flooded with a large number of messages. I quickly perused the pending messages, prioritised them for the convenience of my operators who had been working on this link from midnight.

I got a message from Comilla on RR that my CO and Maj Singal OC

Operating Coy with essential signal elements from my Regt were leaving for Dhaka by 7.00 am. I had thought about this requirement; there was a small unit accommodation adjoining the Signal Centre building, with a few barracks meant for the Signal Centre and Receivers personnel; just outside the Compound. Since a large number of our Army units racing to Dhaka kept pouring and were scrambling for accommodation, I got posted two of our men at the gate to dissuade any of them coming in.

Hav Guldast along with my operator was on the E5 receiver waiting for Calcutta to respond.

Time was 0630 am 18 Dec 1971

(I have already acknowledged the contribution by the Pakistan Corps of Signals' personnel in my article - REMNISCENCES in "The Signalman", April 1972 appended at Appendix 2.)

14

My Tryst with the CSO Eastern Command: 0630 am 18 Dec 1971

Time was a few minutes before 06.30 am, 18 Dec 1971.

Hav Guldast along with my operator was on the E5 receiver waiting for Calcutta Receivers to respond. I was trying to call Calcutta Receivers. I got through to Calcutta Fort Williams Military Exchange. But there was no response from the Receivers. In the meantime, I heard Maj Kataria from the adjoining building frantically shouting,

"Sir, CSO Command is waiting. Please come immediately."

I quickly washed my face and rushed to the Conference Room.

When I entered, I found CSO Command, my CSO, Malay Ghosh and most of the officers who were in attendance the previous evening. They all appeared to have had their rest and in good shape. With my disheveled hair, unshaven face with tired and sleepy eyes, I sure must have looked like a 'scarecrow beaten up by days of rough weather in the field.'

Brig Tiwari gave a stern look. "Didn't you know about this morning 6.30 meeting?"

"No Sir." I replied, "I left immediately after you had given me the tasks."

CSO didn't respond but started the meeting, "Before we proceed, let us have the progress' from Maj Narayanan."

I briefly told the happenings in the past 10 hours, about A7 and how it was put through, about the RR to Comilla and my talk with the SO-in-C, and status of E5; that I was waiting for the call to Calcutta to progress this link when I was asked to come to the conference.

CSO Command; "Our first priority, I thought, was E5 – radio link to Calcutta."

I explained to him that while we could use an existing Rhombic aerial for A7 Delhi, we had to design and install a new dipole aerial for E5 and the efforts made by us and the support from Sub Riaz and Hav Guldast of the Pakistani Signals. I concluded,

> *"Sir, We are through on RR to Calcutta and Delhi. SO-in-C wanted you to call him first thing in the morning."*

Signal Comn ex DHAKA 17/18 Dec 1971 by IV Corps Signals

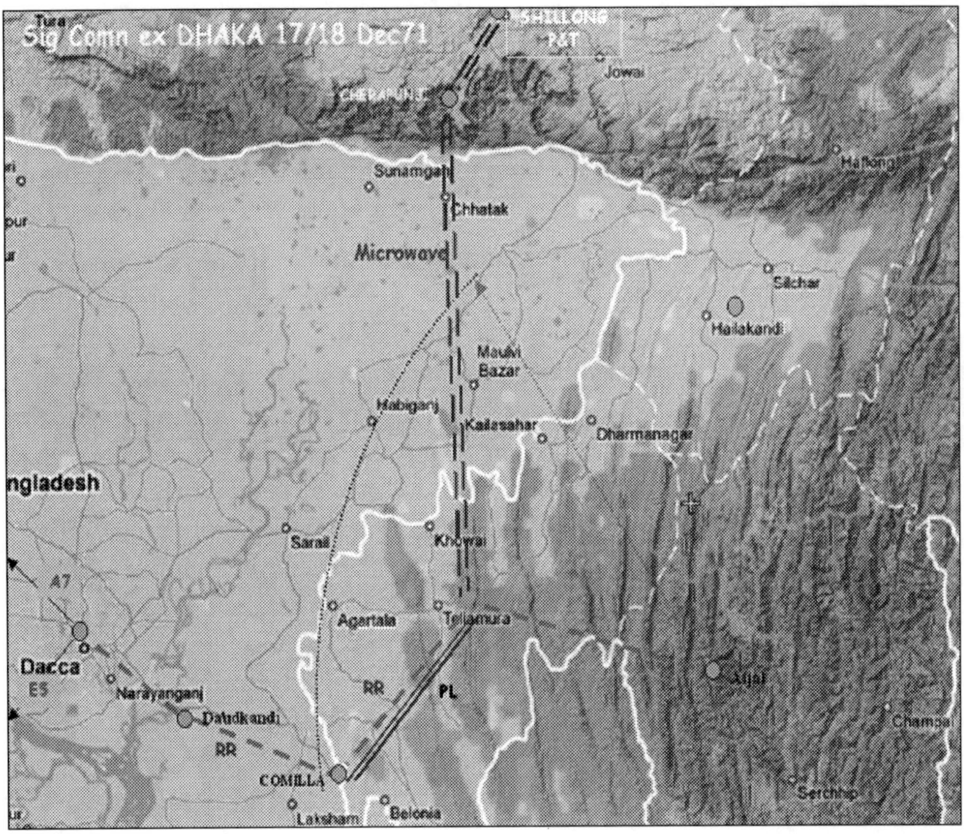

Courtesy Google Map

Brig Tiwari wasn't amused. For whatever may be the reason, he made a strange remark:

> *"If people have been sleeping, how can we put through signal comn?"*

I was deeply hurt. I tried to control my tears and emotions but couldn't help blurting out,

> *"Sir, if someone has been sleeping from this group yesterday night, it was certainly not me; what I have been able to achieve last night, very few signal officers would have been able to achieve under similar circumstances."*

There was pin drop silence for a few seconds. Before Brig Tiwari could say anything, Brig Sidhu quickly came to my rescue,

> *"Sir, Maj Narayanan has carried out the tasks under difficult circumstances, extremely well. I suggest that the Dhaka signal comn should now be taken over by Eastern command Signals." In the same breath, he looked at me and said, "Naru, you better hand over to an officer nominated by the CSO Command."*

The time was 7.15 am, 18 Dec 1971. As I came out of the Meeting, I saw Hav Jadhav. He rushed to tell me that E5 got through at 0630 hrs (immediately after I left for the meeting) and is now functioning well.

I saw my Regimental Sub Major Kehar Singh looking for me. He had just arrived with the advance party that included the langar (cook house) lorry. I guided him to the accommodation already earmarked, adjoining the Signal Centre building. As he was leaving, I said, "Sub Maj Sahib, our detachment personnel had not eaten anything since yesterday evening. Can you arrange for some tea and snacks for all of us including the few Pak Signals jawans who have been working along with us?" In a few minutes, Sub Maj Kehar Singh returned with haversack breakfast (food packets with puri and sabji) and hot tea. This we all shared along with Hav Guldast and the few Pak Signals jawans. Hav Jadhav carried a few packets and tea for the Transmitter Station personnel. I impressed upon him (Sub Maj) that we should take care of these Pak Signals personnel till they are relieved and safely handed over to their PW Camp.

Major Sudarshan Nayar from Eastern Command Signals was the nominated officer by the CSO Command Around 9.00 am, Maj Nayar arrived with one of his JCOs. By then all the comns that we had provided had fully stabilised and there was a spate of calls to Delhi and Calcutta from the two trunk telephones placed in the Dhaka Military Exchange. A7 (RTg) had a number of messages for Delhi. I spent the next couple of hours with Maj Nayar to acquaint him about the signal comn set up at the Receiver and Transmitter stations. I also introduced him to *Sub Riaz, Hav Guldast* and their men from Pak Signals. Maj Nayar promised to relieve them soonest and ensure their safety.

By 12.00 noon on 18 Dec 1971, Eastern Comd Signals through Maj Nayar took over the Signal Comn responsibility at Dhaka from IV Corps Signals.

My CO and other Regiment vehicles arrived by 2.00 pm. And I joined them.

POSTSCRIPT

It is a well-known fact that Brig K K Tiwari, CSO Eastern Command had planned and executed the Eastern Theater Signal comn brilliantly. As per the official War History 1971, Dhaka was not the target in the planning even as late as 1 Dec 1971. Unfortunately, no one expected that Dhaka would fall within a fortnight. Army landline signal comn from Dhaka to Calcutta and Delhi perhaps was also not planned. When Dhaka fell early on 16 Dec 1971, there was no Army derived circuit from Dhaka to cover the surrender on the evening of 16 Dec 1971.

Since the Advance HQ of Eastern Command had organised the historic event, I presume that Eastern Command Signals should have planned the signal comn to Calcutta and Delhi.

HQ IV Corps and IV Corps Signal Regt were still at Comilla then. GOC IV Corps accompanied by the CSO from Comilla had reached Dhaka just at the nick of time on 16 Dec before the historic surrender ceremony held around 4.30 pm. It was only on the following day (17 Dec) I was airlifted to Dhaka in the evening. When I reached, there was still no Army comn. No wonder CSO Eastern Command was upset and, in the process, I had to face all the brunt. All the same, I did not let him down or my CSO and completed the tasks by 0630 am on 18 Dec with utmost professional competence working the whole night and getting the assistance from the Pak Signals personnel (as described in the previous Episodes).

IV Corps elements at Dhaka including advance party of our Regt were ordered to move to Mynamati the following day i.e. 19 Dec 1971.

Brig K K Tiwari visited IV Corps HQ at Mynamati by end Dec 1971. He first came to our Officers' Mess in the morning to meet all the officers of the Regt. He was in a relaxed mood and he made it a point to talk to me and hear more about my exploits at Dhaka on that night 17/18 Dec 1971. I could sense that he was trying to make up for the harsh remarks that he had made.

Not that I expected any expression of regret from such a senior officer. I always had the highest regard for him since my YO days. In fact, he was instrumental in my joining the Corps of Signals. During 1959-60, he was SO1 Signals HQ Eastern Command Lucknow (which later moved to Calcutta) and I was a subaltern (Lt) at Eastern Command Signal Regiment. He picked me up for a special task in Nagaland for security monitoring of the radio nets of the Assam Rifles and Police Battalion and also imparting training in Net Radio Security. Although I was operating from Kohima and Mukokchung, he maintained a hawk's eye on my work and movements. It was during this period under him that I learnt how to be a professional soldier in difficult field conditions. When I returned to Lucknow after 6 months, he made sure that the work that I had done got the recognition.

PART IV

Review, Reflections and Lessons

15

Review and Reflections

The fast and fluid nature of operations conducted by IV Corps under Lt Gen Sagat Singh the GOC was truly remarkable; the operational success has been acknowledged in the official *"War History 1971"* MoD Govt of India (Bharat Rakshak) in these words:

> *"……………The Corps had surprised everyone by its sudden and spectacular crossing of the Meghna. Commanders at all levels showed exemplary initiative and boldness. Lt Gen Sagat Singh GOC IV Corps emerged as the outstanding Corps commander in the entire sub-continent, including the Pakistani Army. It was his initiative, drive and bold decisions backed by meticulous preparations, supported by Eastern Command, which brought his Corps to the gates of Dhaka in sufficient strength."*
>
> **—Fall of Dhaka, Ch 13, p. 572**

IV Corps Signals under Brig G S Sidhu and that included IV Corps Signal Regiment, N Communication Zone Signal Regiment, B Corps Signal Regiment, the signal regiments of the three formations – 8, 23 and 57 Divisions and the Air Support Signal Company assigned to the Corps provided infallible comn during the entire operations.

I was then the engineering company commander of IV Corps Signal Regiment and I have told my story in that capacity. Obviously, the coverage is limited to the extent of my association in the build-up of the Corps backbone comn viz. forward comn to the three Divisional HQ- 8, 23 and 57 Mountain Divisions and rearward comn to Rear IV Corps (Tezpur), Comn Zone (Shillong), HQ Eastern Command (Calcutta) and Army HQ (Delhi).

Contribution by Formation Signal Units

I am fully aware that the three signal units of 8, 23, and 57 Divisions played a major role in the overall signal comn effort. They effectively provided signal comn to the advancing brigades in fast fluid operations once the offensive commenced on 3 Dec. These units were commanded by highly motivated Commanders (Signals) viz. Lt Cols Kalyan Singh (8 Div), Talwar (23 Div) and Chadda (57 Div). I take this opportunity to acknowledge the outstanding contribution made by them and their dedicated signal officers and men towards the liberation of Bangladesh.

I now wish to reflect on the three other Corps signal units:

- N Comn Zone Signal Regiment
- B Corps Signal Regiment
- Air Support Signal Company

N Comn Zone Signal Régiment.

The OC was Lt Col B K Bhandari. Maj J M Khullar was one of the Coy Commanders. The Regiment was responsible to build and maintain hundreds of km of PL in the entire Sector and also take over PL routes owned by the P&T for the Public Call Offices (PCO). He and his unit acquitted themselves most creditably with their untiring efforts in building and maintaining hundreds of km of PL meeting specification standards required for satisfactory functioning of both Army and the DOT carrier equipment. They had provided the backbone PL build up utilising the already available PL routes built by the P&T.

During the thick of the operations, I once asked Col Bhandari, "Sir, how do you contact your officers and det commanders dispersed in such a wide sector and coordinate the efforts." His answer was,

> *"I don't. Instead, they contact me at specified times during the day and definitely once during the night. By that, we ensure timely dissemination of orders, review progress, tie up loose ends etc. We are fighting a war. Every one of my boys understands the importance of being in touch."*

The commitment of the Unit may be gauged from the expeditious manner with which they extended the PL route from Sonamura when the Corps HQ moved to Comilla on the night 11/12 Dec 1971. I just want to recall what I had narrated in Chapter 2.3:

"11 Dec, ... by 11:00 am we had reached Comilla. We deployed the Systems Vehicle next to the Trunk Exchange. To our surprise, the PL route from Sonamura to Comilla had already been patched by our N Comn Zone Signals team led by Maj J M Khullar and by the DET staff at Comilla. What more, they had already tested the Comilla –Sonamura- PL route up to Teliamura. The Carrier and VFT equipment of the P& T type all brand new in our System Vehicle behaved superbly. It is to the credit of IV Corps Signals that even before arrival of the Advance Party, the systems were put through from Comilla to our Teliamura Carrier Centre and a few trunk speech channels were extended beyond to Shillong, Calcutta and Delhi".

B Corps Signal Regiment

This was a new unit ordered for raising sometimes in August 1971 at *Tezpur* to augment IV Corpa Signal resources for the operations. The first Commanding Officer was Lt Col Chakraborty. He was ably assisted by Maj Charan Singh, his 2IC. Charan was also my course mate at the Military College *Dehradun* from where we passed out.

During the period Sep through Nov 71, being ourselves too involved at the op location, we didn't come to know the progress on the raising of the Unit. It was sometimes during mid November 1971, I was taken by a big surprise when 8 nos. of RR detachments complete with personnel and equipment robustly fitted in *unit modified* vehicles arrived at our RR Hill at *Teliamura*. What more, two young officers- Lt Tushar Tamhane (later promoted as Capt) and Lt Tripathy and a couple of JCOs also accompanied. It was only after the War, when we returned to *Tezpur*, I came to know the enormity of their effort, work ethics and professionalism.

We were fully aware that once the formation HQ crossed the IB, our RR comn from Aijal would become marginal. I had planned a RR Node at *Sonamura* much similar to the Aijal node. But, we didn't have any RR terminals, as all these were fully committed on ground. The arrival of 8 RR terminals was most timely; I could now implement establishing the *Sonamura* node. Also, we could afford to group an additional terminal with each of two formations HQ (23 and 57 Div) who would be within RR range from *Sonamura* node. By this, we could cater to both the Main and Tac HQ of these two formations to be in contact with the Corps HQ. In fact, we had even provided the option for them *to hook on* to either Aijal or the *Sonamura / Comilla* node (Grid comn concept) to cater to the formations on Feni–Chittagong axis. But for the silent support from Bravo Corps Signal Regiment, we couldn't have achieved such an innovation.

About the raising of *B Corps Signal Regt* and its role during the 1971 War, I have the pleasure to enclose an article *Reminiscences: Bangladesh War 1971 by Col TD Tamahane, (Retd) at Appendix 3.*

Air Support Signal Company

IV Corps had one company of 2 Air Support Signal Regiment that was located at *Phoolbari* close to *Tezpur* prior to the operations. Maj M A Siddiqui a close friend of mine was the Officer Commanding. On mobilisation, they moved to Teliamura with one divisional section (of 23 Division) and some elements of the Joint Operational Centre staff. The divisional sections with the other two divisions (8 and 57) joined them at the Op location at Teliamura thus completing the full complement for the three divisions of the Corps. At Teliamura, their small unit was co-located with our Regiment. Maj Siddiqui was attached to our officers' mess and had his tent adjoining mine.

During early Sep 71, I was going through a turbulent phase of my Army career after the mishap to the Corps exchange with guilt conscience and feeling of rejection. Maj Siddiqui was the only person with whom I could open up and share my vows. He was very mature and always put me at ease with his comforting words. We always met late in the night to exchange notes on our problems and the future in the face of glorious uncertainties of War.

Maj Siddiqui, himself, was having serious problems as his Company was appallingly short of equipment, secondary batteries for their radio sets and worse still in not having even a full set of tyres for their tentacle vehicles. What more, his detachment personnel were not trained in air support comn procedures. He was obviously facing the heat. Fortunately, during the preparatory phase from Sep till mid Nov 71, he was able to get all the equipment and manpower, trained his unit hard and got his air support tentacle detachments to a high degree of readiness for the operations. By the time the orders came to deploy these with their respective formations sometimes in mid Nov 71, they were fully trained and the morale was high.

Close air support activities commenced on 3 Dec 71 when our troops crossed the IB. The air support net was very effective and ensured speedy and timely delivery of immediate air support demands initiated by the units and formations. Indeed, the Company acquitted itself most creditably during the operations and contributed to the overall success.

Recently (Aug 2008), I had requested Col M A Siddiqui (retired) now settled in Delhi to send a write up on the trials and tribulations faced by him and his Company, how he was able to overcome the various obstacles and managed to successfully provide Signal Comn for close Air Support for the Corps. He responded immediately. His article makes an interesting reading with some very amusing but true incidents and lessons. With his permission, I am including the same at *Appendix 4*.

16

Lessons in Leadership in War or Warlike Situations

While providing infallible signal comn to IV Corps during the Bangladesh War of 1971, there were a number of lessons that had emerged.

When we moved to Teliamura by end Aug 71, the signal comn infrastructure available was primitive; we had to build this up systematically during the preparatory phase over the two months period till end Oct 71. There were vast and diverse Signal resources of the Corps to be deployed on ground to build up the comn network viz. radio, RR, Lines (both PL and field cables) and the associated equipment, power sources like generating sets and battery banks. Hundreds of km of PL had to be built and maintained over and above the already available PL routes owned by the P&T for the civil PCOs. In addition, the formation Signal units had their own PL and cable routes. We also had a vital microwave link from Teliamura to Shillong provided by the P&T to integrate with the National Grid for the Corps rear comn. What more, there were several owners for these, the Corps and the Comn Zone signal units, the signal units integral to the formations under the Corps and the P&T. They had deployed their own line parties and maintenance dets all over the sector. In addition, there were the RR relay stations at isolated locations. All of them needed the logistics support viz. fuel, rations, field maintenance support. Some needed physical security too.

Later during the offensive phase, we had to make use of the captured signal equipment and the comn infrastructure that became available at Comilla and Dhaka. All these called for detailed planning, meticulous execution and close coordination at all levels.

Mantra for Successful Signal Communication

I distinctly remember the first meeting in the CSO's office in early Sep 1971 attended by all Officers Commanding (OsC) of the integral Corps units and Commanders Signals of the Corps formations. It was all about the Corps operational plan and the signal communication build up and challenges. The meeting lasted about an hour; Brig Sidhu appeared to be cool and composed but towards the end he showed his *no-nonsense attitude* when he made it clear what he expected from each one of us:

> *"We are here to fight a War. I expect all of you to function as a team. I do not want any accusations or attempts to let down your sister units or your colleagues. Always remember that:*
>
> *(i) Every communication channel has two ends. Never-ever complain about the other end; instead take responsibility for the other end too;*
>
> *(ii) If a formation is out of comn for more than 24 hrs, I want your best people at the other end".*

Little did I realise then the remarkable power behind the mantra, '*take responsibility for the other end*' implying 'give equal or greater importance to the formation ends.'

Very soon, Brig Sidhu's mantra percolated down to every signal officer in the entire Corps; this had the salutary effect in changing their attitude. Passing the blame to the other end *(other-end-man-ship)* at all levels practically disappeared. What more, there was the attitude of empathy i.e. going out of the way to attend to the needs of the lower formations by sharing essential signal resources and even sparing technical personnel. This helped to cement all the formation signal units under the Corps into a single integrated *'4 Corps Signals Team'*.

Lesson. At senior levels, the focus should be to develop the attitude to assist lower formations and units with essential signal resources and even with your technical personnel; in other words, avoid *hoarding* your signal resources and share what you can with the other end. That is the secret for establishing and maintaining good signal comn.

Upward Delegation

There was yet another attitudinal change that Brig Sidhu brought about in all his officers. I have often heard him say, *"I do not like you coming up to me with problems which you can sort out at your level"*. He thus made it clear that he was totally averse to problems being unnecessarily escalated to him. It was much later at the College of Defence Management (CDM), I came across the term *upward delegation* which means 'referral of problems that can be resolved at your level to your next higher level (your boss) This invariably results in accusations against and attempts to letting down your peers, a tendency most prevalent during peacetime.

Innovation

With the given resources and constraints, one important means to success in any endeavour is the ability to innovate i.e. to think differently to get better or improved solutions.

I honestly believe that our bold and innovative initiative to establish a major RR Comn node at *Aijal* ensured our ability for extended RR comn to the formation HQ in the wide Corps sector. All formation HQ directly under IV Corps had the freedom to move *to any location* within the corps sector (viz. Badarpur, Sylhet-Comilla line, Feni, Chitagong) from where they had to simply *hook* on to the *Aijal Comn node. (Plan AREN concepts still under evolution in those early 70s).* Once the offensive commenced across the IB, our ability to provide comn support from *Comilla* enabled Corps HQ to effectively control the advancing IV Corps formations beyond *Meghna River* and up to the gates of *Dhaka.*

Another innovative solution was at Dhaka Army Transmitter Station where we used the Rhombic Antenna designed for the erstwhile Pak Army *Dhaka-Rawalpindi* radio link for our Delhi A7 Radio link on the night 17/18 Dec 71. These are just a few examples at the functional levels.

Win the Confidence of the Commander and the Staff

As signal officers, we always believed during our days that signal comn are taken for granted and that the commanders and SOs were insensitive to "signals' problems. Perhaps this was true as we had inherited the vintage World War signal equipment and the signal comn were always marginal and under constant scrutiny. In the late 60s and early 70s with the induction of Radio and Radio Relay (RR) equipment indigenously produced by *Bharat Electronics Ltd. (BEL)* and the multi-channel carrier and VFT equipment by *Indian Telephone Industries (ITI),* there was a marked improvement in the quality of comn channels.

The GOC had rightly appreciated that success of the IV Corpa operations would depend to a large extent on good and timely signal comn. Our CSO ensured that the GOC and the Corps staff were fully briefed about the strengths and limitations of the new equipment systems and in particular the effectiveness of RR for duplex voice channels and its range limitations. The GOC's positive attitude to Signals percolated down the chain of command and that ensured better appreciation by commanders and Staff at all levels *of the Signals' problems.*

This brings out a few important lessons.

- At the *Planning and Directional level,* a signal officer should always strive and win the confidence of his commander by his professional competence and ability to deliver; that would ensure his *proactive* involvement right from the planning stage, the signal plan evolved is pragmatic dovetailing into the operational plan and what more, the limitations if any fully appreciated by the commander and the staff.
- At *the execution level,* it is important that the comn facilities provided are robust and the users can make full use of the facilities even if this involves providing them with assistance. During the operations, we had detailed our young signal officers on duty on 24/7 basis in the Ops Room and for manning the Comd Radio Nets. During the thick of operations, when the SOs were extremely stressed and hard pressed for time, they found this arrangement to their liking as that relieved them from their constant need to attend to the net radio with their (clumsy!) RT procedure and marginal speech over RR extended through our vintage manual exchange. This move saved us from many blushes and our young officers did their job well and made us proud.

Coordination of Signals Efforts

It is to the credit of Brig G S Sidhu, the CSO who had emphasised from the very beginning the need for 'close coordination' to ensure optimal deployment and utilisation of the vast and diverse signal resources of the Corps. Another major influence of his was changing the attitude of every Signal officer with his famous Mantra: "Take responsibility for the other end" implying give equal or greater importance to the formation ends.' As a result, passing the blame to the other end (other-end-man-ship) at all levels practically disappeared and there was a healthy interaction from either end to resolve issues at their respective levels (without referral above). What more, there was the attitude of empathy i.e. going out of the way to attend to the needs of others. This helped to cement all the formation signal units under the Corps into one single entity, "IV Corps Signals".

Contributory Factors at the Execution Level

There could be several contributory factors for the success of IV Corps Signals during the Bangladesh war. Based on my personal experience, I have ventured to record a few at the functional (execution level) that I value the most.

I strongly believe that effective coordination at the execution level is achieved by the following three important factors:

- Selection and positioning of the key personnel;
- Delegating responsibility to them; and
- Ensuring fail-safe means to contact them when required.

Delegation permits decentralised execution by your *key personnel* within the framework of the overall Signal plan. It is extremely important that they are briefed about the operations on hand and what is expected of each and every one of them. (*See Note 1*)

Anticipate several steps ahead yet plan for the worst lest you are taken by surprise

When Dhaka fell early on 16 Dec 1971, there was no Army derived circuit from Dhaka to cover the historic surrender on the evening of 16 Dec 1971. Clearly that was an omission at the strategic planning level that took every one in HQ Eastern Command by surprise.

At the execution level, even after detailed planning, we had to anticipate 'where and how things can go wrong.' My experience on the night 6/7 Dec 1971 when we put through a vital RR link to the Tac HQ 23 Div (just in time) taught me this lesson: 'even the best of plans can fail due to human factors and that we should always have a contingency plan that can be executed at short notice.'

Behavioural Dimensions

Attitude Training and Signalmanship

At senior levels, the focus should be to develop the attitude to assist lower formations and units with essential signal resources and even with your technical personnel; in other words, avoid hoarding your signal resources and share what you could with the other end. That is the secret for establishing and maintaining good comn.

At junior levels, for good signal comn, there is need to constantly train our activity level leaders i.e. our YOs, JCOs and NCOs, to imbibe in them '*Signalmanship* or *sound technical practices* like good cable terminations and joints, proper *earthing*, correct radio-tuning drills, properly designed aerials, care and maintenance of the signal equipment, generators and batteries and above all the attitude *"the will to get through."*

Motivation during War

The Corps Commander and the staff were candid in their appreciation for the CSO and his IV Corps Signals team for their major contribution to the success of the operations.

But unfortunately, IV Corps Signals' contribution had not been acknowledged in the official *War History of 1971* or in the *Corps of Signals History* related to this period. Only remark about IV Corps Signals in the *Corps History* appears to be about *the loss of the Corps exchange in the Barak River* just before the Operations *for which I was partly to blame.*

Unsung Heroes

Many deserving signal officers and men who served in the various formation signal units under IV Corps hardly got any recognition in terms of Honours and Awards. *There were many during this operation who had performed exceptionally well beyond their call of duty or the limits of human endurance (or both) but remained* unsung heroes. For this we, the signals officers, are ourselves to blame. Many of us, when it comes to awards and rewards, take our signal warriors for granted. I have often heard these remarks,

> *"What's so special about him to deserve an award? Whatever he has done is as per the normal call of duty".*

Besides such a casual attitude, in a few deserving cases, the IOs (initiating officers) unduly delayed the initiating process; what more, some did not even know the distinction between awards given in war in face of the enemy and those given during the peace time. Perhaps this was the reason why many awards to signals personnel appear to have gone to those serving in the higher static HQ like Calcutta and Delhi rather than those from field formations.

It is our duty as a leader, to make every subordinate feel important and wanted; that he has a role to play; help him to realise what he is doing and what to expect of him. I often recall those early days in Sep 71 after the mishap to the new Corps 200-line exchange and my consequent *face-off with* my CO. I had already resigned myself to my fate (my own imagination) that my Army career was finished. But for my CSO's encouragement and the trust he had shown, I could have ended up as a nervous wreck and been dumped as a 'soldier who failed.' But he made me feel wanted and important. That surely helped me to give out my best during the War.

Delegation of responsibility is one sure way of motivating your **key personnel** to assume responsibilities; when you show confidence in them, it boosts their 'self-confidence' resulting in their taking initiatives; when you encourage the right initiatives that enhance their 'self-esteem'. During War very often you may have to go even beyond your key personnel. For that the Signal plan must percolate down the chain to not only to your Key subordinates but also even down to the level of mechanics and operators, linemen and the drivers since we cannot anticipate when any one among them would become a key person in a critical situation. For instance, recall the incident on the night 6/7 Dec 71 when I had to send my soldier driver Signalman Barkat

Ram with the frequency crystals to Sonamura and restore a vital RR comn just in time resulting in calling off of an operation and thereby save many lives. – see page 36.

Motivation of local population and the POW. I am proud that we were able to get the best out of the civilian staff of the Pakistan Telephone & Telegraph (T&T) at Comilla on the night 11/12 Dec 71 and later on the night 17/18 Dec 71 at Dhaka when we were able to get the captured Pak Signallers helping us to put through vital comn links; all these because of our treating them (locals and the PW) with dignity, winning their trust and confidence and making them feel important.

Awards and Rewards, I wish to reiterate that due emphasis has to be given to the 'attitudinal training' of our signal officers on the aspects of motivation during war; and that includes awards and rewards and the need for the timely initiation. This will ensure that the signals warriors and in particular our junior officers and other ranks (OR) get their due share of awards both during peace and war.

Loyalty during War

In peace, it is prudent to follow the hierarchy; avoid bypassing your immediate superiors. In war, the Nation comes first, always and every time: the organisation you serve comes next; Loyalty to your superior only if the earlier two are not compromised.

It is only after much introspection, have I ventured to reflect my own *'loyalty'* during the operations under three of my role situations viz. to my immediate superior, my peers and my subordinates. This is purely for bringing out some lessons as to how one's attitude gets modified during war or any warlike situation and does not in any way undermine or extol the characters described.

Loyalty to your Superior

During operations, I had my immediate boss in *Lt Col Harkrishan,* my CO who was also my IO and whose appraisal report would decide my future Army career.

Because of my *face-off* with my CO during the early days in Sep 1971, I couldn't effectively share my views on the comn matters freely with him. Due to intense operational pressures, very often I was constrained to interact with SO2 Signals on vital comn matters and sometimes directly with the CSO amounting to bypassing my CO. Thus, I was at conflict within myself to contend with my own conscience on my *'loyalty'*. It was during this period, *Aijal RR node* was approved by the CSO based on my suggestion much to the discomfiture of my CO. I had to rationalise with the thought, "after all we are fighting a war and for providing vital comn, my loyalty has to be first to my Corps." Time being the essence, I believed that I could make such exceptions and not strictly follow the hierarchy.

When the RR node started to function, my CO realised that it was the right decision. Thereafter, he never interfered nor questioned my judgment. He also accepted the fact that between Malay (SO 2 Signals) and me, we could resolve all problems in regard to *'Resources to Tasks'* without any compromise to the Corps Signal Plan. My CO, therefore, was prudent enough not to make this an issue. His only directive was to keep him briefed. I recall these words of his," Naru, I know you are busy the whole day and you do have a lot of interaction with the SO2 Signals (Malay Ghosh). That's good. But keep me informed at the earliest. Call me even if it is midnight." Later he fully supported the Move of Corps HQ to Comilla 11/12 Dec 71 night based on his full confidence in our ability to deliver.

Loyalty to your Peer

'Loyalty' is what you expect from your juniors and give to your superiors; but to your peers, you have to consciously develop such an attitude. Over my long years in the Army and later in the corporate world, I have noted with much regret that attitudinal development of 'loyalty' to your peers has not been given the due importance. I would now like to dwell on an altogether different aspect of loyalty behaviour in two types of peer situations, one while dealing with a peer who you perceive as directly competing with you and the second with an empowered peer because of his proximity to higher superior officer.

Loyalty to Competing or Empowered Peer

I am not aware of this aspect of human behaviour being explicitly discussed in any Management or Human Behaviour related literature. I strongly believe that such a loyalty belongs to an altogether different class of superior human behaviour that manifests more during War or in the face of adversity.

Let me explain with the following two examples.

My peer in competition during the operations was Maj I C Singal, the other senior major (besides me) posted to my Regiment to earn criteria appraisal report (for promotion to Lt Col.). Ishwar was a diligent, extremely hardworking and a mature officer. He was the OC Operating Company responsible for the Corps Exchange and the Signal Centre to handle the voice (local and trunk) and telegraph circuits. In this capacity, he acquitted himself most creditably. During the crucial preparatory phase from Sep through first week of Dec 1971, we both decided to share the same-tented accommodation-a fairly spacious store tent. That helped us in our developing a close rapport, mutual respect and appreciating each other's operational needs and constraints. By this, we could resolve a number of problems or issues among ourselves without referral above (or upward delegation).

After the War, during March 1972, I happened to travel with my CO who was proceeding on posting to Army HQ Delhi. During our conversation, *Lt Col Harkrishan* made one very significant observation, "Naru, I expected many times that you or Ishwar would try to let down each other. Fortunately, you both were very mature and never indulged in that."

Empowered peer is a Staff Officer (SO) in the higher formation HQ under whom your unit has been placed. During peacetime, I have seen quite a few SOs taking undue advantage of their position and even creating a wedge between the CSO and the COs and other senior unit officers.

During the War, my empowered peer was Maj Malay Ghosh, SO2 Signals. Since the SO1 Signals was in the Rear IV Corps HQ at Tezpur most of the time, for all communication related matters, we had to deal with Malay.

Malay was not only intelligent and competent, but had sterling soldierly qualities. He had the total confidence of the CSO and commanded respect of the Corps staff. He played the important role in cementing all the formation signal units directly under into a homogenous team. He discussed all the 'Resource to task' issues with the unit commanders and the officer's concerned and gave the right advice to the CSO before signal plans were finalised.

For me, he was my most dependable colleague. I owe him for much of the success that we had achieved as part of IV Corps Signals during the operations. It was only after reaching Teliamura on 3 Sep 1971 that I could meet and interact with him. We had some of the finest professional moments during those crucial months. Malay always discussed with me the Corps signal plans and new commitments to get my reaction from implementation point of view. We did have some serious differences on some issues but all these were in the larger interests of providing timely and reliable Corps comn. The CSO always encouraged our interactions. That helped us to *synergise* our efforts and arrive at some bold and innovative decisions and solutions. For instance, move of the Corps HQ to Comilla on the night 11/12 Dec 71 was as a result of our forward planning, validating the resource availability on ground and meticulous execution thus living up to trust and expectations of the CSO to deliver. What more, on 11 Dec, when the advance elements of the Corps HQ moved to Comilla, he willingly assumed the comn responsibility at the Comilla end to oversee taking over of the Comilla Exchange from the DET and engineering of the rearward communications till he was relieved by Maj I C Singal of our Regiment later.

Loyalty to your Subordinates

Loyalty is not one-way traffic. If one expects loyalty from his subordinate, he has to reciprocate too; that is the trait of a true leader and shows his integrity and courage. I often recall the incident when my CSO stoutly defended me during my *tryst with CSO Eastern Comd* on that early morning of 18 Dec 71 at Dhaka.

Besides several other means of showing your loyalty to your juniors, during War one sure way is by ensuring that deserving cases (in particular the junior officers, JCOs and men) get the recognition that they deserve. That is possible by taking appropriate initiation actions without bias or delay. I had recommended the names of two of my Young officers, two JCOs and one OR immediately after the War. The recommendations in respect of the two YOs were withheld by the CO (the IO). Both JCOs got awards *(Mentioned in Dispatches)*; that helped Sub Maj Kalidas to get an honorary rank of *Lt* and Nb Sub Natu to progress in his Army career; he got a specialist commission and rose to the rank of a *Col* before he retired.

But the two YOs didn't progress much in their career although during the War they had shown promise and the potential for growth. Getting an award that too in War at that stage surely would have done wonders in enhancing their self-esteem and confidence and perhaps motivated them to perform better in their career. As I look back, I should *have fought for their cause* but I didn't as I myself was struggling with the system that I believed was faulty.

I strongly urge you the reader to reminisce your own experience in these different role situations to pause and introspect. Would your conscience endorse your 'loyalty' or would it point an accusing finger at you?

Lessons Pertaining to Character and Attitude

I have summed up below some of the lessons pertaining to the character and attitudinal dimensions that I had absorbed during the War. I strongly believe that these are applicable to every service officer be he from the Army, Air Force or the Navy. I was fortunate to imbibe some of these and practice with a good measure of success both during my career in the Army and in the corporate sector post retirement.

Communication

Every comn channel has two ends. Never complain about the other end at any time. Instead develop the attitude to take responsibility for the other end also. A deeper examination of the mantra, 'take responsibility for the other end' would reveal that it is relevant to non-signal comn too, both verbal and non-verbal and to every walk of life whether inter-personal or organisational. Successful comn (relationship) can be expected on most occasions if the comn channel remains open.

Loyalty

In peace, it is prudent to follow the hierarchy; avoid bypassing your immediate superiors.

In war, the Nation comes first, always and every time: the organisation you serve comes next. Loyalty to your superior is only if these two are not compromised

Convictions and Duty

A modified interpretation of "Karma Yoga" for Service Offrs: Do your duty without worrying about the outcome; but have the conviction of what you are doing is right and in the best interests of your organisation. Also learn to preserve yourself in positions of influence to enable you do what you believe is right. In other words, "for doing good, learn to swim along with the sharks".

Risk Taker vs. Risk Avoider

In peace, because of the very nature of our tenure and appraisal (reporting) system, majority of our service officers prefer to be 'Risk Avoider'.

In War, you should be a 'Risk Taker' capable of taking calculated risks based on sound professional judgment. You are sure to succeed and earn the respect of your superiors, peers and your subordinates.

Image

Both in peace and war, your suggestions will be respected only if you have the right image. Build that image with your professional competence and the ability to take calculated risks. It is ongoing process at every stage of your professional career.

Anticipation

During war (or hostile environment), anticipate several steps ahead; yet plan for the worst lest you are taken by surprise

Adverse Situation to your Advantage

Develop the attitude to look at every adverse situation as an opportunity and take full advantage.

NOTE

1 We had grouped one RR terminal with each formation. Normally a Hav or a Naik commands a RR detachment. However, for the RR terminals grouped with the formations, I had attached an officer or a JCO for better coordination and response. This was also in line with my CSO's directions to ensure best efforts at the other end. They were fully briefed about the Signal plan and their role and what was expected of them. This decision proved to be most effective later during fast fluid operations when the formation HQ moved frequently.

I have cited below two examples:

- We had made Sub Natu in charge of the Systems Vehicle ably assisted by Hav Jadhav. They showed remarkable initiative when they moved with the Systems vehicle to Comilla and engineered the rear comn on the early morning of 11 Dec 71. See Ch 3.1
- For the Dhaka-Comilla RR Link, we had planned a relay station at Daudkandi and made Capt Tamhane in charge. The young officer showed a lot of initiative in deploying his RR relay station at Daudkandi (unmindful of Pak soldiers still in that area retreating to Mynamati. He kept a constant vigil the whole night of 17/18 Dec waiting for the RR Signal from Dhaka. When we finally did come up, he responded instantaneously and facilitated the rear comn link up. That made telephonic comn possible with Army HQ (Delhi), and the Eastern Comd HQ (Calcutta). See Ch 3.3 and Appendix 4 - Reminiscences Bangladesh War 1971 by Col (retd.) T D Tamahane

Conclusion

By mid-Jan 1972, IV Corps HQ and all the Corps units returned to their peace location and we came back to Tezpur.

Corps of Signals Day was due on 15 Feb 1972 and we were determined to make it most memorable. There were a number of festivities for our troops and we had also organised a grand evening function at our officers' mess that was attended by all the senior officers in the Station including the civilian dignitaries. *Lt Gen Sagat Singh, our GOC* made a memorable speech expressing his deep appreciation for the CSO and his IV Corps Signals team, for their major contribution to the success of the IV Corps operations. Here is an excerpt from that speech: (Full transcript of the speech on that occasion is given at Appendix 5).

> *"... Comn never-never failed.... May I gratefully on behalf of the entire Corps, the fighting Corps, submit that we couldn't have achieved the success that we did, had it not been for Brigadier Sidhu, IV Corps Signal Regiment, B Corps Signal Regiment, N Comn Zone Signal Regiment. Frankly, I couldn't have achieved the success had it not been for their support and for their efficiency.... ".*

'Indeed the *'Sparrows of IV Corps Signals flew like eagles'* during the 1971 battle for the liberation of Bangladesh'.

"They that wait upon the Lord shall renew their strength;
They shall mount up with ***wings as eagles****; they shall run, and not be weary;*
and they shall walk, and not faint."

— *The Bible*

Epilogue

Post Bangladesh War-1971, I developed greater confidence in all aspects of 'operational comn'; I grew progressively in stature and gained wider recognition.

In 1979, when I was a Lt Col, I was nominated on the prestigious "Higher Defence Management Course" (HDMC), an essential stepping stone to rise in service. This course is run at the College of Defence Management (CDM) – an inter Services Institution for imparting management training meant for its senior officers in the reckoning for higher ranks like brigadier and major general. I was retained on the faculty of the CDM and got the 'cdm' tag added to my name.

In my last assignment from 1985 to 1988 as a Brigadier, I held the prestigious appointment of Project Director Plan AREN under the Ministry of Defence for modernising the field force comn. In 1987, I was also approved for promotion to the rank of Major General along with just two others from my batch of over a dozen Brigadiers. I, however, had to retire as a Brigadier in July 1988 due to lack of a vacancy, a paradox, that within two weeks after my retirement, two officers, one above and one below me on the seniority list got promoted.

I was thus a good loser once again. But that gave me the *opportunity* to enter the corporate world. Public Enterprises Selection Board (PESB) selected me as CEO of Central Electronics Ltd. (CEL)-India's pioneer in solar photovoltaic (SPV). On superannuating, I became a professional consultant in 1994 to Indian Renewable Energy Development Agency under the Ministry of Non-Conventional Energy Sources and got an opportunity to do project study for the World Bank.

Since 1998, I have been an Adjunct Professor at Birla Institute of Technology and Science, Pilani, guiding the engineering students in their *final semester* internship training in electronics and IT companies at Bangalore, thus keeping my interest in these areas sustained.

It was at the College of Defence Management, when I was a Colonel, I was able to understand and appreciate the psychological dimensions of motivation and my own 'Need Achievement' profile. Whereas that enabled me to reach certain growth levels in my career, I realised that I lacked that 'Need Power' instinct to attain positions of higher authority and influence. I realise, at my present age of 85 (2019), that I should have developed the 'Need Power' ambition without compromising the tenets of 'Karma Yoga of Bhagavat Gita' interpreted in my own way thus:

> ***Conviction and Duty**: Do your duty without worrying about the outcome; but have the conviction of what you are doing is right and in the best interests of your organisation. Also, learn to preserve yourself to attain positions of authority and influence to enable you do what you believe is right. In other words, "for doing good, learn to swim along with the sharks".*

Acknowledgements and Gratitude

I wish to acknowledge the special debt that I owe to Brig G S Sidhu, AVSM who was CSO IV Corps during the 1971 War; for reviewing the early drafts of my book, for the counsel, advice and motivation and above all corroborating with many of the critical events narrated. My special debt is also due to my colleague Lt Gen M K Ghosh, PVSM, (former SO-in-C) who was then the SO2 Signals IV Corps; for the empathy and support that he gave me during the 1971 War and for reviewing my draft and add 'his side of the story' to give an insight into the 'Signals Planning' during the early preparatory phase in July-August 71 and later during the Corps offensive phase from 3 Dec till 11 Dec 71. I also owe to Cols M A Siddiqui, Arjun Deva and T D Tamhane (now retired) for sharing their experiences during the 1971 War to corroborate and 'value-add' to my story.

In October 2008, I had the l first full draft of my book "When Sparrows Flew like Eagles" sent to Lt Gen Y S Panwar, AVSM, VSM, the then Commandant of Military College of Telecomn Engineering (MCTE) for his perusal and review. He made a very encouraging comment that how my book would be useful to our signal officers at the young officers' and middle management levels. He also skilfully edited the text, tidying up the inconsistencies and pointing out inaccuracies and suggesting improvements.

Due to reasons beyond my control, my book remained unpublished for long years mainly due to my deteriorating health with Leukemia (Blood Cancer) which prevented me from actively pursuing with my efforts to publish the book.

In July 2019, I made a resolve to get the same published during my lifetime. I revisited my earlier draft, tried to substantially improve the contents, particularly to make it a training document to bring out useful lessons on human behaviour under extreme stress and leadership lessons to service officers at functional, middle and top management levels in war or warlike situations. For this very reason, I strongly believe that these lessons in leadership would be equally relevant to the corporate world in adverse business environment.

I owe my gratitude to the Ministry of Defence, Govt. of India (Bharat Rakshak) for use of a few excerpts selectively from the "*War History 1971,*" to corroborate events that relate to sig comn efforts. I also wish to acknowledge use of Google Maps pertaining to the operational sector of IV Corps in 1971 for suitably superimposing the sig comn sketches to make them more realistic. All these have been shown at the appropriate paras/sketches in the Text.

I am grateful to Mrs. Asha Uberoy, wife of Brig D K Uberoy, Signals for motivating me at this late age of mine to get the book published for posterity and for taking the responsibility for all pre and post publication activities. My special thanks are due to Director, United Service Institution of India (USI) for agreeing to publish the book under the aegis of USI.

Last but not the least, my gratitude to Shantha, my wife who has steadfastly stood by me for the past over 55 years since our marriage including that crucial year during the 1971 War when I was away engaged in operational duty in the war zone.

APPENDICES

APPENDIX 1

Indo-Pakistani War of 1971

(Extracts from Wikipedia, the free encyclopaedia)

Indo-Pakistani War of 1971
Part of the Indo-Pakistani Wars

Lt Gen A.A.K. Niazi signs the instrument of surrender on Dec 16, surrendering his forces to Lt. Gen Jagjit Singh Aurora.

Date	Dec 3-Dec 16, 1971
Location	Current day Bangladesh and Indian-Pakistani western border
Result	Pakistani forces in the East surrender unconditionally to Mitro Bahini; Victory of the Indian Armed Forces in the Western Theatre.
Territorial changes	Bangladesh becomes an independent state.

The Indo-Pakistani War of 1971 was a major conflict between India and Pakistan. The war is closely associated with Bangladesh Liberation War (sometimes also referred to as Pakistani Civil War). There is an argument about exact dates of the war. However, hostilities commenced officially between India and Pakistan on the evening of Dec 3, 1971. The armed conflict on India's western front during the period between 3 Dec 1971 and 16 Dec 1971 is called the Indo-Pakistani War by both the Bangladeshi and Indian armies. The war ended in a defeat for the Pakistani military after being faced on two fronts.

The Indo-Pakistani conflict was sparked by the Bangladesh Liberation war, a conflict between the traditionally dominant West Pakistanis and the majority East Pakistanis. This gave India a strong advantage over Pakistan. The war ignited after the 1970 Pakistani election, in which the East Pakistani Awami League won 167 of 169 seats in East Pakistan, thus securing a simple majority in the 313-seat lower house of the Majlis-e-Shoora (Parliament of Pakistan). Awami League leader Sheikh Mujibur Rahman presented Six Points and claimed the right to form the government. After the leader of the Pakistan People's Party, Zulfikar Ali Bhutto, refused to give premiership of Pakistan to Mujibur, President Yahya Khan called in the military, which was made up largely of West Pakistanis.

Mass arrests of dissidents began, and attempts were made to disarm East Pakistani soldiers and police. After several days of strikes and non-cooperation movements, Pakistani military cracked down on Dhaka on the night of March 25, 1971. The Awami League was banished, and many members fled into exile in India. Mujib was arrested and taken to West Pakistan.

On 27 March 1971, Ziaur Rahman, a rebellious major in the Pakistani army, declared the independence of Bangladesh on behalf of Mujibur. In April, exiled Awami League leaders formed a government-in-exile in Boiddonathtola of Meherpur. The East Pakistan Rifles, an elite paramilitary force, defected to the rebellion. A guerrilla troop of civilians, the Mukti Bahini, was formed to help the Bangladesh Army.

On 27 March 1971, the Prime Minister of India, Indira Gandhi, expressed full support of her government to the Bangladeshi struggle for independence. The Bangladesh-India border was opened to allow the Bangladeshi Refugees safe shelter in India. The governments of

West Bengal, Bihar, Assam, Meghalaya and Tripura established refugee camps along the border. Exiled Bangladeshi army officers and voluntary workers from India immediately started using these camps for the recruitment and training of Mukti Bahini guerrillas.

As the violence in East Pakistan escalated, an estimated 10 million refugees fled to India, causing financial hardship and instability in the country. The United States, a long and close ally of Pakistan, promised to ship arms and supplies to West Pakistan.

Indira Gandhi launched a diplomatic offensive in the early autumn of 1971 touring Europe, and was successful in getting both the United Kingdom and France to break with the United States, and block any pro-Pakistan directives in the United Nations security council. Gandhi's greatest coup was on 9 August when she signed a twenty-year treaty of friendship and co-operation with the Soviet Union, greatly shocking the United States, and decreasing the possibility that the People's Republic of China would become involved in the conflict. China, an ally of Pakistan, had been providing moral support, but little military aid, and did not advance troops to its border with India.

Operation of the Mukti Bahini caused severe casualties to the Pakistani Army, which was in control of all district headquarters. As the flow of refugees swelled to a tide, the economic costs for India began to escalate. India began providing support including weapons and training for the Mukti Bahini. By Nov, war seemed inevitable; a massive buildup of Indian forces on the border with East Pakistan had begun. The Indian military waited for winter, when the drier ground would make for easier operations and Himalayan passes would be closed by snow, preventing any Chinese intervention. On 23 Nov, Yahya Khan declared a state of emergency in all of Pakistan and told his people to prepare for war.

On the evening of Sunday, 3 Dec, the Pakistani air force launched sorties on eight airfields in north-western India. This attack was inspired by the Arab-Israeli Six Day War and the success of the Israeli preemptive strike. At, 5:30 PM that day, General Yahya Khan ordered the Pakistan Air Force to bomb Indian Forward Airbases. Pakistan started flying sorties towards India within fifteen minutes of the order. Pakistan launched attacks against eight Indian airfields on the Western front including Agra, which was 300 miles (480 km) from the border. These attacks could only achieve partial success. Unlike the Israeli attack on Arab airbases in 1967, which involved a large number of Israeli planes, Pakistan flew no more than 50 planes to India. Indian runways were non-functional for several hours after the attack. But these attacks gave India a good reason to launch an attack against Pakistan. India started flying sorties to Pakistan by midnight. On the Eastern front, the Indian Army joined forces with the Mukti Bahini to form the *Mitro Bahini* ("Allied Forces"); the next day the Indian forces responded with a massive coordinated air, sea, and land assault on the West Pakistani Army in East Pakistan.

Yahya Khan counter-attacked India in the West in an attempt to capture territory, which might have been used to bargain for territory they expected to lose in the east. The land battle in the West was crucial for any hope of preserving a united Pakistan. The Pakistan Army faced a crushing defeat at Battle of Longewala, where a 2000-3000 strong assault force of the 51st Infantry Brigade of the Pakistani Army- backed by the 22nd Armoured Regiment was kept on hold by the Indian 'A' company of 120 odd soldiers of the 23rd Bn, Punjab Regiment. The Indian Army quickly responded to the Pakistan Army's movements in the west and made some initial gains, including capturing around 5,500 square miles (14,000 km^2) of Pakistan territory (land gained by India in Pakistani Kashmir and the Pakistani Punjab sector were later ceded in the Simla Agreement of 1972, as a gesture of goodwill).

At sea, the Indian Navy proved its superiority by the success of Operation Trident, the name given to the attack on Karachi's port. It also resulted in the destruction of 2 Pakistani destroyers and a minesweeper, and was followed by the similar Operation Python. The waters in the east were also secured by the Indian Navy. The Indian Air Force conducted 4,000 sorties in the west while its counterpart, the PAF put up little retaliation, partly because of the paucity of non-Bengali technical personnel. This lack of retaliation has also been attributed to the deliberate decision of the PAF High Command to cut its losses as it had already incurred huge losses in the conflict. [2] In the east, the small air contingent of Pakistan Air Force No. 14 Sqn was destroyed resulting in Indian air superiority in the east. The entire campaign was a true blitzkrieg, exploiting weakness in the enemy's positions and bypassing opposition, resulting in a swift victory.[3] Faced with insurmountable losses, the Pakistani military capitulated in just under a fortnight. On Dec 16, the Pakistani forces in East Pakistan surrendered. The next day India announced a unilateral ceasefire, to which Pakistan agreed.

The war led to the immediate surrender of Pakistani forces to the allied forces of India and Bangladesh, jointly known as the Mitro Bahini. Bangladesh became an independent nation, and the third most populous Muslim country. Loss of East Pakistan demoralised the Pakistani military and Yahya Khan resigned, to be replaced by Zulfiqar Ali Bhutto. Mujibur Rahman was released from West Pakistani prison and returned to Dhaka on January 10, 1972.

APPENDIX 2

Remniscences

By

Maj M R Narayanan

(Article by the author in April 1972 just after the 1971 Bangladesh War in the Corps of Signals Magazine *"THE SIGNALMAN",*)

So much has already been said about the role of Corps of Signals during Operation "Cactus Lily." Indeed, the Corps has contributed in no small measure to the success of the operation. It is at this hour of glory that I wish to record some of my own recollections of those events that made history.

I was associated with the operations from the very beginning. By the first week of Sept 71 we had concentrated at our new location, a primitive and under-developed area from comn point of view. Incessant rains further intensified the problem of settling down. It was at this juncture that our SO in C and the CSO Eastern Command visited our location to see for themselves what was happening. Needless to say, that their visit acted as great morale booster. I cannot forget that wonderful gesture on the part of our SO in C when he departed with these words to my CO, "Well Harkrishan, you and your boys are doing a good job under difficult conditions. Keep it up."

"Our line circuits started stabilising and the P and T staff also started working with some purpose. The Corps Exchange started functioning with a modest 50 lines CB non-multiple-board. At this stage a mishap saw our 200-line CBM Board go into the river with its vehicle while boarding a ferry. Although the vehicle was recovered, the exchange was badly damaged. I was to a certain extent involved in this unfortunate incident, as I happened to be the convoy commander of that ill-fated convoy.

During early Oct 71, it was thought that at all levels that radio nets should continue to rest and that the queen of the ionosphere should not be disturbed from her deep slumber. On 14 Oct 71, she had to be awakened abruptly. My radio boys who till then, were only playing a passive role, were suddenly inducted into the proceedings. We were asked to open and see 'through' as many as six medium power radio links that night.

It was indeed heartening to see these young officers, JCOs and other ranks rising to the occasion. Lt Tarun Kumar Mahendra and his team worked the whole night and by morning an inhospitable piece of land had been converted into an efficient elegant looking "radio village" consisting mostly of Siemens's 400-Watt mobile stations with their typical "triple folded dipole" aerials.

The "radio village" became the centre of hectic activity during the remaining period till 11 Dec 71, when we had to move to our new location.

As was to be expected, RR proved to be the most effective and reliable means of comn during the actual operations. The staff was shy of speaking over Radio and this naturally increased the strain on our RR. Initially we had provided a single relay RR chain for each division. However, as the operations progressed, this had to be supplemented by 'Grid' system that catered for both Main and Tac HQ. This ensured that one of the HQ was always in touch.

An incident on the night 6/7 Dec is worth mentioning. The tactical HQ of the Division was moved during day and our RR detachment also moved with it. It was appreciated that the relay location had to be changed to a new location about 30 Km away. The corps commander always spoke to the divisional commander every morning and it was imperative that we put through the RR link before 5 am. Naib Subedar Dinkar Natu who had moved forward with the relay station did not come up on the air and we were getting anxious. At 10 pm, he came up on the line to say that he was through to the Tac HQ on RR but that he had some problem with the rear RR link to us. The speech was too faint. What surprised me was from where he got the line as no line existed to the relay location. Anyway, this was not the time for such irrelevant questions. The main concern was to see the Corps Commander's call through as usual and this was done. Subsequently, I came to know from Nb Sub Natu that Maj J M Khullar whose line parties were working in that area extended the line from an existing PL route to the relay location. Jimmy that night worked with a great presence of mind. He had to divert the route he was constructing, but he did it although it involved additional work for him and his linemen. But for this, I shudder to think what the result would have been with the Division out of comn with the Corps for more than 6 hours during that crucial period.

Throughout the operations, we had to work in close coordination with the P&T staff. In a small improvised tin shed the corps carrier complex had to be built-up in pouring rain. It is to the credit of my Line Carrier Section under the leadership of Sub Maj Kalidas that a seemingly impossible task was completed. By the middle of Nov 71, our embryo carrier centre had grown in stature to become full-fledged and biggest carrier station in Tripura for about 22 carrier channels and an equal number of VFT channels. It was a matter of pride for me to be associated with this carrier station while more often than not the entire P&T systems were manned by my company mechanics – Hav Jadhav and his dedicated team.

My story would be incomplete without mention of my association with the Pakistani Signal Corps. After the Pakistani surrender on 16 Dec 71, I flew by helicopter to Dhaka on the 17th Dec. It was late in the evening when the CSO called me and said," Naru, the SO in C desires a RTg circuit from Dhaka to Delhi. It will be a shame on us if we cannot put through the Delhi RTg circuit." Luckily I spotted Sub Riaz and Hav Guldaast (Pak Signallers) at the Transmitter Station. Both of them were most cooperative and worked the whole night with me to commission one of the existing 1 KW transmitter and sort out the remote-control lines. They bore no malice or ill will against us. When I asked them why they had not damaged the equipment, Guldast replied, "Sir, I have been with these transmitters for the past 1½ years. I have not seen anything else during this period. How can I destroy these equipments, which are as dear to me as my own children?" The same night, we were realigning one of the feeder routes and I suspected there might be mines in the aerial park. Sub Riaz told me, "Sir, I promise you there are no mines in this area. If you want, I will walk ahead of you." By late night, we were ready and the Delhi RTg link was established. Needless to say, events of the night 17/18 Dec 71 have been the most memorable ones to me during the entire operations.

The operations are now over and as I write these recollections in the prevailing lull after the battle, I am confronted with the big question, "when again we are going to get similar opportunity, the challenge, the adventure, and the thrill Op Cactus Lily offered us?" I say to myself, "Well there may be many more occasions in the future but none as unique as Cactus Lily that has helped to establish the new nation of Bangladesh, raised the stature of our own country, upheld the prestige of our armed forces, and above all enhanced the reputation of our Corps."

'THE SIGNALMAN', APRIL 1972

APPENDIX 3

Reminiscences: Bangladesh War 1971

By

Col TD Tamhane (Retd)

About Myself

I graduated from the National Defence Academy, Khadakvasla and the Indian Military Academy, Dehra Dun and was commissioned into the Corps of Signals on 21 Dec 1968. On completion of the mandatory young officers' course at MCTE, Mhow, I was posted to Q Comn Zone Signal Regiment (now the E Composite Signal Regiment).

The unit's responsibility was to provide signal comn to formations earmarked for operations in the Western Theatre. The peacetime activity, therefore, was primarily to train for all types of contingencies that could arise in War or Warlike situations.

I was inducted into the unit as OC RR section, where I had the privilege of being trained by my Company Commander *Maj MSH Jahangir*, a meticulous officer who taught me the nuances of RR path profiling to work out the best site for RR communication. *Sub Bhagat* was my mentor for practical handling of the vintage but reliable RS C 41/R222 and ACT (1+4)3A and detachment training in establishing a RR station to include RR site selection, erection of aerials, tuning of the equipment, deriving the carrier channels and most importantly extending the channels to the Exchange. The rigorous training that we went through under the watchful eyes of our CO, Col. RG Singh, stood me *in good stead* during the 1971 War for the liberation of Bangladesh.

Prelude to the 1971 Operations

The year 1971 was eventful as the clouds of war were building up. It is an inherent desire, of all young officers like me to participate in at least one war during their career in the Army. A flurry of postings started pouring in, and *lo and behold* my posting order arrived to ***Bravo Signal Regt,*** *a* unit *under new raising just before the war.* It was with mixed feelings that I received my posting; on the one hand was this golden opportunity to get war experience and on the other hand was the concern and anxiety of my parents when they hear of my move for operations.

The posting was forthwith hence there was no time to muse over it. The process of handing over was indeed harrowing as there were numerous queries to settle, and to my horror I found that my commanding officer Col. NC Achaia refused to sign my clearance. I got a shock of my life, as my bag and baggage were already loaded in the train and I was standing before the CO to be relieved. I was finally told to push off with a warning not to miss my train. I just about managed to reach the station and was bundled into the train that was already in motion. I could see the agony on the face of my parents, who had specially come to see off their son proceeding for War in the Eastern Theatre.

Preparatory Phase

Bravo Signal Regiment was a new raising, specifically designed for providing signal communications to a mobile Corps. The new raising took place at Tezpur within the premises of IV Corps Signal Regiment (bulk of whom had already moved to Teliamura in Tripura State on mobilisation). Col Chakraborty was our commanding officer with Maj Charan Singh supporting him as second in command. The experience of a new raising is unique; personnel flowed in by hordes and they had to be accounted for. Non-compliance of posting orders was required to be reported; stock was to be taken of all new men posted in by numbers rather than by name which is the normal procedure of new raisings. The incoming manpower had to be screened and posted to the various companies and sections depending upon their trade, experience, and potential. In flow of vehicles, stores and equipment commenced as a trickle initially and ended in a flood. There were very large number of GS vehicles that were issued in lieu of specialist vehicles. Innovation was the name of the game, to modify these vehicles suitable for housing the signal equipment and make them function as comn vehicles. We had to literally race against time to be ready for the impending operations. On my part, with all the ingenuity, I managed to get the RR vehicles ready for the operational role.

By mid Nov 71, we were ready and devoted the next few days to practice detachment drills to hone the skills of the RR detachments, viz. to site a RR vehicle, position the transmit and receive antennae correctly so as to prevent interference, erecting the same in the shortest time, tuning of RS C41/R222 and aligning the carrier equipment; we also paid attention to the usual battle drills for organising the defence of the detachment as a part of the overall defence of the supported formation or independently as a relay station.

One of the brighter sides of war or war like situation is getting higher responsibility due to shortage of officers; Yes, I was promoted to the rank of Captain with just 3 years of service. 'How proud I felt that day when my CO and 2IC placed the Capt's badges of rank each on one shoulder of mine simultaneously'.

Bravo Signal Regiment, being a new unit under raising, did not get the opportunity to function as a fully integrated communication unit with its supported formation. The operational task assigned was to supplement the resources of the integral IV Corps Signal Regiment; the RR Section of Bravo Signal Regiment was, therefore, placed under IV Corps Signal Regiment and we were to function under Maj Narayanan Officer Commanding the Engineering Company of IV Corps Signal Regiment. Captain Nirmal Dhillon was the RR Section Commander.

Around mid Nov 71, we were ordered to move to the 'Concentration Area' of HQ IV Corps at Teliamura. Since Radio silence had been imposed, we did not get adequate time to test our radio equipment on live RR links and had to depend entirely on our acquired skills during the training and exercises in our previous units. However, in the short time that was available, our RR dets were imparted limited training and marrying up with those of our host unit.

In the last week of Nov 71, I was assigned the task of providing RR communication to 23 Mtn Division (the spearhead division of IV Corps). I along with my RR terminals reported to 23 Mtn Div Sig Regt at Kakraban. The CO of the Regt, Lt Col Talwar asked his Officer in Charge

Signal Centre- Capt GC Sharma to update me on the operational situation and my role to provide the rear RR link to the IV Corps HQ at Teliamura.

On the morning of 3 Dec 1971, we were all awaiting the 'word go' for the offensive and fully set to provide RR comn support

The Offensive

The code word to launch the offensive was given and the leading brigade firmed in at Bhadarpur. Orders for the move of the *Advance HQ* of the Division to Bhadarpur were given. We queued up in the order of march of the *Advance HQ* by mid night and awaited our turn to move. Finally, at dawn, we moved into East Pakistan from the North. There were scattered firing and we were given protection by the HQ protection unit. After a number of halts due to sporadic enemy action, we finally reached Badarpur at night.

Siting of the RR Det definitely posed problems. Darkness, unfamiliar terrain and uncertainty of area being clear of mines were our major concerns. Being flat ground, it was difficult to select a site with FFZ (RLOS) clearance. A quick *reconnaissance* and interaction with the staff of the Advance HQ and ascertaining the location of the Signal Centre complex, I set about the task of selecting the site and ordering deployment of the RR Det. We did get through with the Corps HQ with maximum aerial height, but the RF was marginal and was not adequate for mounting of the carrier equipment (ACT (1+4)3A). A two-way (duplex) audio patch was extended to the exchange, owing to the urgency of the situation, and a warning that all calls being processed should be unclassified. Later the Divisional HQ moved to Chittagong from Bhadarpur, and we successfully put through the RR communications.

RR Comn to Dhaka after Surrender on 16 Dec: RR relay at Daudkandi

On 17 Dec in the afternoon at Comilla, Maj Narayanan tasked me to establish a RR relay at Daudkandi on east bank of Meghna River by 1800 hours (17 Dec) and be on the listening watch awaiting RR signal from him from Dhaka. Daudkandi was a ferry site where a pontoon bridge was established to cross the river, enroute to Dhaka. I moved the RR dets to Daudkandi and reached destination well before sun set; this helped in establishing the relay station. Since the bridge site was on the river bank it was not suitable for obtaining the required (FFZ clearance). I didn't want to take a chance of setting up a marginal RR link; I scouted the area and located a mound. It was about a km away from the bridge site and lacked inherent defence and fire support from our troops at the pontoon bridge site; but was ideally suited for RR communications. The RR link to Comilla was established without problems. The RR terminal to establish the link to Dhaka was tuned and kept ready and we were on listening watch as per instructions.

Having completed our primary task, I set about to co-ordinate defences, being detached from the protection of the bridge-head. After earmarking the defensive perimeter fire trenches, I proceeded to the bridge site and informed them of our location and the purpose of our being there; we then arranged mutual support between each other. During this period, I saw a large movement of Pak troops fully armed, which made me warn men to be on guard and alert. I had, thus, completed my task well in time and we patiently waited for the RR det Dhaka to come on air. Around mid-night (17 Dec), the RF monitor showed a flicker, all personnel in the det were alert and anxious. As soon as the radio was tuned, Maj Narayanan came up on the air. It was a pleasure listening to him. I did query him on the delay. He explained the situation at his (Dhaka) end; he congratulated the efforts of our relay dets. After the radio patch was extended from Dhaka to Comilla, we breathed a sigh of relief, on successful accomplishment of our mission.

Liberation of Bangladesh and Return of the Indian Army

Post 16 Dec 1971, with the surrender of Pak Army in East Pakistan the new nation 'Bangladesh', was born. The task of IV Corps Signals at Mynamati was to assist civil administration to establish communications. The RR dets of the Bravo Signal Regiment were to fall back to Mynamati and were placed along with Signal elements of 23 Mountain Division Signal Regiment to oversee the communications. The line detachments of N Comn Signal Regiment and Bravo Signal Regt continued to stay at Mynamati for restoring the PL.

Convoys of vehicles of troops commenced move, initiating the withdrawal of Indian Army from Bangladesh. We watched them move out with envy. However, very soon, the rear parties of 23 Mountain Division started thinning out. Along with them, we were also ordered to move back to Tezpur.

I, with my RR detachments, commenced move to re-join parent unit- Bravo Sig Regt. This move was an experience; I have heard the saying *'an army marches on its belly'*. How true it was. Since we were last in the return schedule, the administrative support in the form of rations, fuel, Repair and Recovery, vehicle maintenance was totally lacking and we were left to fend for ourselves. We even had to load a couple of generator trailers into a 3 Ton GS vehicle, as towing these was difficult over narrow roads in the hilly terrain with hairpin bends.

The annoying process of peace time accounting on cessation of war, such as Station Orders for attachments normally taken care of by the unit QM, was learnt the hard way. However, it was an interesting experience. Everyone was eager to help, but the audit requirements of peace time accounting necessitated following the lengthy procedures.

In the process of joining our parent unit at Tezpur, I learnt a bitter lesson that haste must be resorted to as the last option. We were short of rations for the last leg of our move from Guwahati to Tezpur; hence I decided to put Sub Bhagat, my second in command, in charge of the convoy and I was to bring up the rear collecting the stragglers; vehicles that had broken down, having pulling problems and otherwise unserviceable after the war were to be safely brought home. The decision to look after the welfare of the men under my command by not delaying the entire convoy *back fired* as one of our RR vehicles met with a fatal accident. It resulted in the death of one of our radio mechanic Sigmn RM Yadav, serious injury to the driver and minor injuries to the two other members of the det. This was the only casualty suffered by Bravo Sig Regt during the 1971 Operations on the Eastern Front.

Conclusion

The victory on the Eastern Front was not the end of the Indo–Pak War of 1971. The urgent need for the signal resources in the Western Theatre required Bravo Signal Regt to move to J&K. Just before the actual move, my posting to NDA on a forthwith basis had arrived. My move to Pune coincided with the move of the Regt. I was given a pleasant surprise when officers of my Regt came to the New Bongaingaon railway station at midnight to bid me a farewell.

POSTSCRIPT

I have tried to recount events to the best of my ability after 36 long years. At that time, I did not realise the importance of maintaining a diary, especially during the war. However, the sequence of events is in a chronological order.

APPENDIX 4

Air Support Signal Comn in IV Corps during the 1971 Bangladesh War

By
Col M A Siddiqui, (Retd)

Introduction

1. During 1971, I was Officer Commanding 1 Company, 2 Air Support Signal Regiment. The company was with IV Corps, located at Phulbari, in district Tezpur, Assam. When we were ordered to move with the Corps for the operations, we were told to leave behind a skeleton Joint Operations Centre staff and the Division section allocated to 17 Mountain Division. On arrival, at the destination, the two Divisional sections which were permanently with 8 and 57 Mountain Divisions were to join us, thus completing our full complement for the three Divisions that were to be with IV Corps.

2. While the Division section that was with 57 Mountain Division, was in reasonable shape as far as equipment, vehicles and manpower was concerned, the section that was with 8 Mountain Division, left much to be desired. The operators of this section having been permanently with the Division Signal Regiment did not know air support procedures at all. Their equipment was in bad shape, with no secondary batteries for their radio sets and not even complete tyres for their tentacle vehicles. There were 14 tyres for the four 1-ton tentacle vehicles. The result was that they *leap frogged* while coming to join us from Zakhama, in Nagaland, where the Division was stationed. Two tentacles would cover 50 km distance at a time and then take a halt while the tyres of one vehicle were removed and taken back so that the remaining two vehicles could join them. They, thus, took a whole week to reach.

Preparation for Operations

3. We were short of secondary batteries. The Deputy Director Ordnance with Headquarters IV Corps suggested that we do local purchase and buy civilian lorry batteries from the local market. We needed something like 100 odd batteries which we could not buy from Agartala, the nearest town, as the local dealers simply refused to follow the army procedures where they got payment much later after they had made the supply. The spirit which we generally see in places like Punjab was lacking amongst the locals, who were very indifferent to what was happening around them. Besides, there would have been problem with the battery terminals as well, since some modification was also needed to be carried out to the battery connectors of radio sets, to enable use of vehicle batteries. I accidently came to know that 57 Mountain Division Signal Regiment, which I had the privilege of commanding much later, were planning to back load to Ordnance depot, a large number of new batteries which were not even given the initial charge. I promptly got the transfer orders for those batteries to our unit. Now was the problem of how to give them the initial charge. In normal time, this is an EME responsibility but our workshop simply refused saying that they did not have the requisite infrastructure to do this job in field conditions.

4. We decided to initial charge the batteries ourselves but we did not know from where to get the sulphuric acid to make the electrolyte? I asked our Regiment in Calcutta to buy acid from local market. I arranged for it to be airlifted to our field location. Maj RS Chhikara, an old friend was the GSO2 Operations (Air), at the Command Headquarters and very helpful. I had specifically asked the Regiment to see that they did not buy electrolyte as I already collected enough distilled water (thanks to the incessant rains that we had) and we would make our own electrolyte once we got the acid. Alas, when the consignment arrived, we found that they had sent to us electrolyte instead. We followed the same process again and finally got our acid requirement. We were thus able to solve our battery problem.

Training in Air Support Procedure

5. Since the personnel from other divisional sections which joined us in situ, were not trained in air support procedures, we re-formed detachments by posting personnel from within our unit, so that every tentacle had at least one trained operator. We carried out intensive training of operators to make them fully conversant and trained in procedures. We were lucky that we had two full months' time to carry out preparatory activities. We managed to bring all detachments to a very high degree of readiness for the operations. By the time the orders came to deploy the air support tentacle detachments with their respective formations, our confidence and morale was high.

Ground to Air Communications

6. Initially, the radio set that we had for ground to air communications for the air observation post, was BE 201 which used secondary batteries. The set was vehicle bound and not suitable for any man pack use. Before operations were to start, we received the new portable sets, GU 734, which used portable NiCad batteries. We received 14 sets, four each for the three Division sections and two at the Joint Operations Centre. Out of four frequencies made available to us, one was an international frequency and another open for civil use. This left us with only two reliable operational frequencies. Therefore, it was decided by the Command HQ that new frequencies would be allotted. The crystals for these new frequencies were received by the EME workshop, which was to fit them in these sets. On a Sunday, Brig GS Sidhu, our CSO asked me to meet him in the DD EME's hut and bring a radio set GU 734 along. There, the DD EME demonstrated the process involved in the change of crystals, a task which would normally be carried out at the base workshop only. He explained it as a very simple process and within the capability of the local EME workshop. In the process of demonstration however, I realised that this set had become faulty and later, when we took the radio set to the workshop, they simply refused to look at it saying that they had no literature or expertise to repair it.

7. By mid-November 71, all our tentacles detachments were already deployed with their respective forward formations. One day, the SO1 (Signals) Corps Headquarters called me and said that orders for the new frequencies have come and are to be implemented. For this new crystal sets had to be installed in our GU 734 radio sets. I told the SO1 that it was impossible as the sets were already deployed with the formations. The SO1 then suggested a novel method of getting the crystals replaced. I was told to withdraw sets from one formation, get the replacement incorporated and then do the same with the second formation and finally the third one. In his estimate, we could do this in a few days' time. When I firmly told him that I cannot carry out the task as suggested by him as it was impractical, he told me that it was an order and I simply had to implement it.

8. I then went to the 5 TAC Commander, Gp Capt Gopalan and told him about the orders that I had received, stating that I can promise no ground to air communications, in the event of hostilities breaking out, as we will have our formations on different frequencies, not compatible with those fitted in the aircraft. His reply was " Look Siddiqui, it has already been confirmed by your Command Headquarters to Headquarters Eastern Air Command that they are ready with new frequencies to operate and based on this all our ac have already been fitted with new frequencies. What do you expect me to do at this stage?" My reply was "Sir, your aircraft are at their bases but my sets are deployed with the forward formations in the field, where technical support for replacement of the crystals is not available. Therefore, I am unable to implement the orders that have been given by our Signals Branch". Unluckily, the CSO was also away at that time and I could not seek his help. The TAC Commander understood my problem and spoke to the CSO Eastern Air Command, that we are not ready yet for the new frequencies. Their order to the bases was thus reversed and all the aircraft were asked to switch back to old frequencies. We were thus able to avoid a major disaster, as air support to the ground troops, played a very significant role in the entire Bangla Desh operations and our communications never failed.

The First Day of Operations

9. The first offensive by 23 Division on Akhaura, a railway station on Pak side of the border, was to go in the next day i.e., 4 Dec. Air strike demand was made and the ETOT was being repeatedly postponed by IAF. The Corps Commander decided that if the air strike was not forthcoming, our troops were to go in without it. Finally, two Hunters aircraft were sent from Bagdogra on strike mission to us. However, instead of going towards Akhaura, the aircraft headed for Sylhet which was on 8 Mountain Division front. Since aircraft were way off the planned target, contact with the air op could not be made. We at the TAC Headquarters could hear the conversation between the two Hunter pilots, when due lack of communication with the ground force they finally decided to head back to their base. On their return path as they were approaching from a wrong direction towards own troops, the AF Radar station at Shillong declared our own Hunters as hostile aircraft. The news of hostile aircraft in the air created a panic at the Joint Operations Centre, as we assumed that the warning coming from the radar station at Shillong meant that Pakistan's Sabres were coming to neutralise our Hunters. The TAC Commander said, "Siddiqui do something, we must warn our pilots of the presence of the hostile aircraft. The Hunters would be sitting ducks for the Pakistani Sabres". I told him that I had a GU-734 with me. He could make a transmission to warn our pilots, but we were located in a depression and it was highly unlikely that the pilots would hear our transmission. Just then, we saw the Hunters fly past our location. We realised that what we thought to be hostile aircraft were our own Hunters. One could see a visible relief on the face of TAC Commander. These Hunters were the same which came for our mission but went to a wrong location.

Communications with INS Vikrant and Romeo Force

10. INS Vikrant was in the Bay of Bengal and joined our net on the fourth day of the operations. An immediate air strike demand was raised by the Corps Headquarters to INS Vikrant. For some reason, INS Vikrant went off from our net and we could not pass the message to it. I informed the GSO1 Operations, at the Corps

Headquarters of our inability to pass the message. The reply I got was, "Look Siddiqui, when the GOC asks you Signallers, you say through Sir. It is your problem how you pass this message and put the phone down". I was in a fix what to do. I thought for some time, and then called the Signal officer at the Naval Establishment in Calcutta to find out if he had any communication with the ship. He confirmed he was through, and I dictated the message to him on the telephone itself. The message was passed and the ETOT was received in the same way and the air strike materialised at the specified time. Later, when the ship joined the net, we enquired the reason for their being off the air. We were told that a fire accident had damaged their equipment and hence they were not in the air.

11. Romeo Force was an amphibious force created on an adhoc basis and our Regiment in Calcutta had given them a radio detachment. They followed no procedures and we were through with them only occasionally. Not much action also took place in their area of op.

XX Mountain Brigade Heli-borne Operations

12. Maj JL Puri, an old friend was the OC I Company in 8 Mountain Divisional Signal Regiment. While I could visit all our tentacle detachments with other formations, which were within easy travel time, I could not do this with the tentacles deployed with 8 Mountain Division. I was keen to visit and see in what state they were and requested the CSO for a lift in a helicopter which was visiting the area. I, thus, went along with the Corps Commander when he visited Headquarters 8 Mountain Division. I met Maj Puri and saw my boys to perk up their morale. Their minor administrative problem I could solve with Puri's help. I was in regular touch with Puri, but when they planned the heli-borne operation of XX Mountain Brigade, I was not informed. The result was that the tentacle detachment with this Brigade carried the bulky C11/R210 radio set with two secondary batteries and a generator for the operations. They were in the first wave which came under heavy enemy fire, could not land, and came back. One soldier was hit by a bullet and died. This had visibly shaken Naik Raju, who was the detachment commander and it took a lot of persuasion

and pep talk from Puri to build up his morale when the detachment was sent again in the next wave.

13. I only came to know of this the next day, when I found this tentacle going off the air frequently. I then called Puri and came to know what had happened. Had they informed me, I could have requested the CSO to loan us HM 30 sets which are portable HF sets and use NiCad batteries. A few sets were with Corps Signal Regiment. However, this detachment performed very creditably. The C11/R210 radio set of the air support tentacle was their only means of communication with outside world, as the HF set that was sent to work on the D1 net of 8 Mountain Division, had battery problem and could not get through. In order to conserve batteries, I told Naik Raju, to open the set only when he had a message to pass. They could not start the gen set to charge the batteries as the noise immediately drew enemy fire. He thus was able to remain on the D1 net of the Formation and provide crucial communications to them, apart from switching back to our net to pass air support demand messages. As many as six immediate air support demands were initiated by the heli-borne forces and all of them materialised, thanks to our communications which just kept going. Later, when I met this detachment, I found them to be in very high spirits for the task they had so well executed. I had recommended a high gallantry award for Naik Raju and I think he got 'Mention in Despatches'.

Conclusion

During the last few days of the operations, the race as to who would reach Dacca first was a priority and the rearward communications were given a go by. There were times when our tentacle was the only means of communications with the formations. I was thus told by the CSO to keep our communications going and not to switch off our sets. There was also a time when our tentacle set was commandeered by a brigade Signal officer for his own communications when his set became faulty. We took these things in our stride. Now, when I sit back and reminisce the days gone by, a feeling of satisfaction creeps into me. I am grateful to my officers, Maj Shashi Mishra and 2Lt SS Gill and men for their unflinching support, which enabled our unit to perform well.

APPENDIX 5

Transcript of the Speech by Lt Gen Sagat Singh, GOC IV Corps: Signals Anniversary – Feb 72

Ladies and Gentlemen,

Today is the Corps of Signals Day. I have conveyed my felicitations to all members of the Corps of Signals in IV Corps. But this celebration tonight, soon after our victory in Bangladesh, is of special significance. On this occasion, I feel obliged to acknowledge gratefully all that the Corps of Signals led by Brigadier Sidhu did for IV Corps during the operations. I may sound emotional but I may confess and claim, I was not so in operations. I was a harsh man, I didn't spare myself, I didn't expect anybody to be spared, whether a rifleman, a signalman or a gunner or whether he was an EME man.

The fact, Ladies and gentlemen is this, IV Corps did a historic advance of 110 miles, over five water obstacles, of which the MEGHNA was the widest water obstacle. Military History books record the crossing of the RHINE. May I submit to you, RHINE is one third of the water obstacle of the MEGHNA. MEGHNA is two times wider than the BRAMHAPUTRA that you know here in TEZPUR. However, that's a matter apart; a matter of topography. The Corps responsibility, lay from North of SYLHET down to COX'S BAZAR and the whole of MIZO HILLS; all of which I think is a great geographical mass. I couldn't have exercised my operational command, had it not been for Brigadier SIDHU and his resources. He never failed me. He was entirely in my confidence I would tell him, GURDIAL this is what's in my mind, and he wouldn't ask me any questions at all He rose to every occasion-every demand; comn never-never failed. I don't think there is any parallel in History where a Corps Headquarters moved within enemy gun shells as we moved into Comilla. And we couldn't possibly have moved there, unless Brigadier SIDHU and his Corps of Signals had ensured our comn. Now this is something, Ladies and Gentlemen, a fact of history and undeniable. The whole Corps Headquarters moved on the night of 11/12 Dec and we couldn't have functioned there, if we had not gone ahead and established the comn within enemy gun range. May I gratefully on behalf of the entire Corps, the fighting Corps, submit that we couldn't have achieved the success that we did, had it not been Brigadier SIDHU, IV Corps Signal Regiment, B Corps Signal Regiment, N Comn Zone Signal Regiment. Frankly, I couldn't have achieved the success had it not been for their support and for their efficiency. I am most grateful. Thank you, Brigadier SIDHU.

Bibliography

1. Extracts from Wikipedia, the free encyclopedia. **"Indo-Pakistani War of 1971."**

2. *Maj M R Narayanan.* **"REMNISCENCES"** *The Signalman, Corps of Signals Magazine April 1972.*

Index

About the Author

Brig M R Narayanan, VSM is a retired Corps of Signals Officer. Over a span of the 31 years that he served in the Indian Army, he had held a number of challenging appointments at both directional and conceptual levels in particular post-Bangladesh War 1971. Narayanan was known in the Corps for his technical competence and his ability in applying his technical knowledge innovatively in various situations of war at a Corps level. He was also an Instructor at the college of Defence Management where he had honed his management skills. In his last assignment as a Brigadier he was Project Director Plan AREN for modernising the field force communications.

Post retirement, he joined the Public Sector as Chairman & Managing Director of Central Electronics Ltd. (CEL). He was also consultant to the Ministry of Non-Conventional Energy Sources (MNES) when he did a few project studies awarded by the World Bank. He was on the faculty of Birla Institute of Technology and Science (BITS) Pilani as an Adjunct Professor for the students' internship training in Electronics and IT at Bangalore.

He wrote his story, *"When Sparrows flew like Eagles"* in 2008 when he was past 74 years of age about his experience during the 1971 Bangladesh War when he was a Major while serving in the IV Corps Sector. He has applied his vast experience both in the Army and in the Corporate world to draw a number of Leadership lessons for war or warlike situations that are equally applicable to adverse business environment.